Low Maintenance Gardening

By the Editors of Sunset Books and Sunset Magazine

LANE BOOKS • MENLO PARK, CALIFORNIA

Acknowledgments: Without the help of landscape architects and designers, educators, ornamental horticulturists, and directors of prominent public gardens throughout the nation, the intensive research needed for this book could not have been accomplished. A valuable source of ideas and early direction was Josephine Willrodt, Redwood City, California. Others whose help was freely given include Mai Arbegast, Berkeley; Dr. Wolford B. Baker, Emory University; Ernesta A. Ballard and Julie Morris, Pennsylvania Horticultural Society; Philip Chandler, Santa Monica; Webster Crowley, Morton Arboretum, Illinois; Bill Evans, Walt Disney World, Florida; Dr. James R. Feucht, Colorado State University; O'Neil Ford, San Antonio; Fred C. Galle, Callaway Gardens, Georgia; Dr. William G. Gambill, Jr., Denver Botanic Gardens; Eric Golby, Bradenton, Florida; James F. Griffin, Jr., Florida Nurserymen and Growers Association, Inc.; Dr. A. C. Hildreth, Littleton, Colorado; Dr. Warren Jones, University of Arizona; Henry M. Lambert, Dallas; Frederick McGourty, Jr., Brooklyn Botanic Garden; Lois Paul, Longwood Gardens, Pennsylvania; Richard Pope, Sr. and Robert Kunz, Cypress Gardens, Florida; Dr. Kent Schekel, Washington State University; Dr. William C. Welch, Texas A. & M. University; and Ernest Wertheim, San Francisco.

The many professionals who contributed to the unique garden plan chapter are identified on page 15.

Supervising Editor: Robert G. Bander

Research and Text: Elizabeth A. Porter and Patricia Hart Clifford
Special Consultant: Roy Rydell, landscape architect, A.S.L.A.
Illustrations: E. D. Bills (pages 8-13; 16-51)
               Vern Koski (pages 2; 15; 53-60)
Design: John Flack, JoAnn Masaoka
Cover Photograph: Ells Marugg

Executive Editor, Sunset Books: David E. Clark
First Printing March 1974

Contents

Introduction:

How to Have an Attractive Garden on Your Own Terms

If you're expecting this to be an "I Hate to Garden" book, better stop right here. Because it isn't. This is a book for people who like gardens and gardening—but on their own terms. It's directed to the man who values his putter and driver at least as much as he does his rake and shovel.

It speaks to the woman whose interests may take her in many directions—child shuttling, volunteer services, antique hunting, career scouting. Read on, though, if you're a gardener who wants to surround himself with attractive growing things but does not want to put in much time to make them flourish. For you, low maintenance gardening may be the answer.

Let nature do its thing

Low maintenance gardening has a lot in common with organic gardening: both approaches emphasize the vital but often overlooked role of *nature* in gardening.

Keep nature's favorites—the native plants from your region—in the front of your mind as you read this book. In some cases, they are the "Open Sesame" to carefree gardening, enabling you more nearly to attain that low maintenance ideal of a no-care garden.

Drive around your surrounding countryside to observe those native trees and shrubs that thrive without attention from anyone. Some of these may well be good candidates for your garden. Many such natives from all regions of the country are listed in this book, but ask your local nurseryman for names of others. Often, natives are not commonly sold commercially but can be specially ordered.

NATURAL GARDEN, only few steps from house, features shady, secluded deck in an oak and redwood grove. Minimum landscaping of wild ginger preserves the woody atmosphere.

CONSTRUCTED GARDENS *are sure step toward minimum care.* **Left:** *cobblestone-on-concrete blocks set in sand curve past junipers, replace demanding planting beds. Landscape architect: Roy Rydell.*
Below: *combination of wood, exposed uggregate, dichondra, and rocks give Oriental cast to rear yard.*

What this book isn't . . . and is

It's probably easier to say what this low maintenance gardening book is *not* than what it *is*. It isn't:

- A cure-all for every garden problem.
- A "magic" list of plants to fulfill all of your esthetic desires with no care whatsoever.
- A sheaf of suggestions that will allow you to go away for extended periods and forget your garden.
- An "anti-gardening" book designed to eliminate all gardening chores.

None of these things does this low maintenance gardening book attempt to offer. But, you may ask, "What *is* low maintenance gardening, then?"

It's planning. In order to create a low maintenance garden, you must be willing to give some initial time and thought to the planning stages of your garden. Repeated throughout the text of this book is the phrase, "Take time to plan in the beginning." With careful planning and development, you'll soon have a garden that is a source of pleasure and relaxation instead of constant irritation.

Before rushing out into the yard on a Saturday morning with your spade and clippers, sit down at the kitchen table with an extra cup of coffee, a paper and pencil, and your gardening book. Plan first.

It's knowledge. Low maintenance gardening is gardening with a knowledge of the proper techniques. This is a book that offers such techniques as mulching to keep down weeds and watering and planting to minimize pruning and plant failure. Perhaps, for the first time, you'll be able to get ahead of garden chores. And the preventive way of dealing with your garden problems is often the best way for a low maintenance gardener.

It's choosing wisely. Selecting hardy plants suitable to your climate, planting a ground cover instead of a lawn, choosing perennials for color instead of annuals, placing drought-resistant plants where watering is difficult—these are among the low maintenance choices this book can help you make.

It's balance. As you think about some of your favorite garden pleasures, consider what is most important to

THREE WAYS to lessen garden chores are shown here. **Left:** *use native plants as transition between natural landscape and your driveway. Left foreground, Mugho pine; right, Yucca flaccida fit well in Boise, Idaho, setting.* **Top right:** *cactus, yucca, rocks, sculpture form Palm Springs succulent oasis.* **Bottom right:** *Japanese sand garden contains volcanic rocks, sand traced in various pleasing patterns.*

TURN YOUR high maintenance swimming pool into a low maintenance water garden (left). This one in San Rafael, California, contains carp that keep down algae from water lilies and cyperus diffusus. Below: a gardener's dream—a friendly raccoon to regularly trim garden edges. (Water garden idea by Dennis C. Muir.)

you in relation to the time and energy you have to invest. A mass of brightly colored annuals or a rose garden may be high maintenance to one person, whereas to another it is a source of pleasure—a way to relax and get out-of-doors—and therefore not a maintenance problem at all.

It's relying on labor-saving devices. Taking advantage of gardening gadgets to save time and work is another aspect of low maintenance gardening. Your garden tool supply should be adequate, well-organized, and stored properly so you can have easy access to the right tool when you need it. Such labor-saving devices as timers and moisture indicators for sprinkling systems will also save you a great deal of work.

It's being flexible. Just because you may have grown up in a tradition of expansive green lawns, foundation shrub plantings, beds bursting with annuals, and meticulous perennial borders doesn't mean that you're locked into such a garden pattern for the rest of your life. Some wonderful effects are achieved with a *garden of native plants*—accepting the wild flowers, shrubs, and trees that have naturally grown up on your property and making the most of them, rather than leveling your lot and beginning anew. Introducing to your garden plants native to your area can also guarantee low maintenance.

Some adventuresome homeowners explore the possibilities of a *constructed garden*—a garden that has few growing plants in it but instead relies upon paving, fencing, tile, gravel, rock, statuary, and other garden art for color, texture, and effect.

Another possible approach to low maintenance gardening is the *sand garden* of Japan. A bed of smooth sand, patterned in an abstract way with lines and curves and perhaps punctuated with a few rocks or bonsai trees, is a stunning—and relatively carefree—sight.

In areas with warm climates and well-drained soil, a *succulent garden* can offer a striking, low maintenance alternative for the overburdened gardener.

For you: leisure without guilt

Low maintenance gardening, then, is accomplishing the *most* gardening with the *least* effort. It is *not*:
- Mowing vast expanses of lawn each weekend and hand-trimming around the edges.
- Slashing your way through an overgrown jungle of a back yard in a desperate pruning effort.
- Finding your favorite plants riddled from chewing insects or prostrate from unknown causes.
- Covering your front yard with gravel and a birdbath.

Low maintenance *is* mastering the art of "benign neglect." Planned carefully for low maintenance, your garden will be happy and attractive for a considerable period of time with or without you in it. You'll have the freedom to take off for a weekend of boating or skiing, and your garden will survive your absence.

When you begin to feel comfortable in your garden, when you feel you've really come to terms with it, then you can be reasonably sure that you're gardening in the low maintenance way.

Landscaping for Relaxed Gardening

Would you recognize a low maintenance garden if you saw one? One clue might be the absence of a gardener, sleeves rolled up, hoeing away at stubborn weeds. Another might be a pleasing combination of trees, shrubs, ground covers, paving, and construction. Still another clue might be a station wagon pulling away from the driveway, its roof rack stacked with weekend camping equipment. If none of these clues works, this book may become your best ally in recognizing—*and*

in achieving—a low maintenance garden situation.

On the following six pages, you'll see gardens—and parts of gardens—that, for one reason or another, require minimum care. Whether you live in the city or in the country, on a flat lot or on a hillside, in coldest Minnesota or in most tropical Florida—you can surround yourself with greenery and inviting outdoor living areas that require little upkeep if you follow the principles that are pictured and described on the pages to come.

HOUSTON, TEXAS: Slow-growing plants in this formal courtyard need little pruning. Finials at corners of treillage are echoed by potted blooms at corners of fountain and statuary at base of tree, giving garden a classic European look. Plants: 1. Cherry laurel 2. Azaleas 3. Japanese boxwood 4. Southern live oak 5. Aspidistra 6. Star jasmine. Landscape architect: Gregory Catlow.

FORT COLLINS, COLORADO: This rear garden is stocked primarily with easy plants. Tumbled rocks beside artificial stream conceal layer of polyethylene plastic that has been laid to eliminate garden weeds. Plants: 1. Mugho pine 2. Columbine 3. Sedum 4. Daylily 5. Cottonwood trees. Landscape architect: Chris G. Moritz.

LOS ANGELES, CALIFORNIA: *The walk to the house takes you through a woodsy glade. All the plants are grown for year-round greenness and lush performance in the shade.* **Plants: 1.** *Wild strawberry* **2.** *Leatherleaf fern* **3.** *Sycamore* **4.** *Native oak.*

GREAT NECK, NEW YORK: *A garden pool and hardy plants with a Japanese air create a woodland setting that requires little care.* **Plants:**
1. Japanese maple 2. Yew (Taxus media) 3. Azaleas 4. Epimedium 5. Swiss stone pine 6. Junipers 7. Canada hemlock 8. Cotoneaster 9. Ajuga 10. Big blue lily turf 11. Heartleaf bergenia 12. Umbrella pine. Landscape designer: Rudi Harbauer.

GIG HARBOR, WASHINGTON: *Brick paving flush with the lawn creates a mowing strip to make lawn care easier. Hollowed-out cedar logs serve both as dramatic accents and unusual containers for tough but delicate looking plants.* **Plants: 1.** *Saxifrage* **2.** *Sedum* **3.** *Sempervivum.* *Designer: Doug Verbonus.*

TUCSON, ARIZONA: *A simple design sets off the strong character of these plants. A gravel mulch cuts down on maintenance and helps to re-create a natural desert setting.* **Plants:** *1. Soaptree yucca 2. Lavender cotton 3. California fan palm.*

OAKLAND, CALIFORNIA: *Ground covers and curving lines soften concrete paving. Steps were poured in redwood headers and brushed to expose aggregate.* **Plants: 1.** *Junipers* **2.** *English ivy.* *Owner-Designer: Peter Gray Scott.*

PALO ALTO, CALIFORNIA: *An old oak shades this front garden which uses shade-loving plants that offer spots of color. Volunteer seedlings are encouraged for a natural, informal look.* **Plants: 1.** *Aucuba* **2.** *Japanese anemone* **3.** *Shrub fuchsia* **4.** *Hebe* **5.** *Camellias* **6.** *Star jasmine* **7.** *Burford holly* **8.** *Loropetalum.* *Landscape architect: Josephine C. Willrodt.*

LONG BEACH, CALIFORNIA: *This redwood plank patio off the living room is surrounded by tropical plants. The necessary moisture is supplied by a hidden sprinkler system.* **Plants:** *1. Bromeliads 2. Philodendrons 3. Ginger 4. Taro.*

...Some Gardens Planned for Minimum Care

PORTLAND, OREGON:
Evergreen plants form a restful background for the spacious patio. Most of the plants contribute a bonus of spectacular bloom as well. **Plants:** *1. Bamboo 2. Heather 3. Azaleas 4. Rhododendron 5. Dogwood.*

ENCINO, CALIFORNIA:
Gazanias offer a soft ground cover, a long bloom season in yellow and orange, and hide litter from the olive tree. Gazanias fill in rapidly, eliminating weeding in that area. **Plants:** *1. Russian olive 2. Gazanias 3. Agapanthus 4. Young redwoods.*

...Still more Carefree Gardens

PHOENIX, ARIZONA: *Plants native to the area practically take care of themselves. Rocks add rugged beauty to the landscape with no care at all.* **Plants:** *1. Creosote bush 2. Cholla 3. Ocotillo 4. Barrel cactus.*

LOS ANGELES, CALIFORNIA: *Big, dramatic plants give this hillside entry a feeling of rustic informality and provide privacy. Owners water monthly and prune just enough to keep plant growth clear of path.* **Plants:** *1. Rosemary 2. African iris 3. Red Australian flax 4. White alder 5. Sugar gum eucalyptus 6. Manna gum. Landscape architect: Thomas C. Moore.*

LAKE OSWEGO, OREGON: *A brick firepit is set in a weed-free, crushed rock surface. A wood seat separates the rock from the cedar chip area behind it, another low care surface.* **Plants:** *1. Douglas fir 2. Viburnum 3. Hybrid blueberries 4. Dove tree. Landscape architect: Chandler Fairbank.*

SAN DIEGO, CALIFORNIA: *Owners traded in their front lawn for a private entry and low care ground covers. Redwood chips fill in between exposed aggregate stepping stones.* **Plants:** *1. Wild strawberry 2. Junipers 3. Ferns 4. Japanese pines.*

Easy-Care Garden Plans-- 60 Variations

"Ideas" is what this book is all about—ideas about low maintenance gardening techniques and hardy plant materials. For if you want to cut down the amount of time you spend working in your garden to make it appealing, you'll need to apply labor-saving short cuts and to know about plants that flourish with little care.

But an important third element also figures in the low maintenance picture: landscape design. Often, a well planned garden can be the greatest help in liberating the home gardener.

This chapter contains low maintenance garden plans created by many nationwide landscape architects and designers. With the goal of providing minimum care gardens, these experts applied their talents to a wide variety of homesite situations. The resulting imaginative explosion on the succeeding pages may intrigue you, surprise you, stimulate you—may even prompt you to ask questions that you never expected to be able to ask. More important, though: these garden plans, carefully examined, will *answer* many of your questions. And by putting these answers to use, you'll soon find that you're spending less time tending your garden and more time enjoying it.

The plans that follow on the next 36 pages are organized into three sections. The first section features a typical rectangular lot (representative of that found in many housing subdivisions) with ten variations on the design theme. In the second section, lots that present particular problems—such as corner lots and hillside lots—appear. In the third section are given before/after designs for specific garden areas (front gardens, rear gardens, and gardens in between).

How can you best put these plans to use? Study them all, not merely the designs from your own region. Even if you're living in Texas, a landscape design from Illinois might suit your house and taste perfectly. You could easily adapt it, filling in with plant materials for your zone that are identified in the charts on pages 64-93.

As you pore over the landscape plans, notice how often differences in regional climate, culture, and general environment affect the design style. For instance, in Florida, the focal point in a rear garden may be a screened-in porch; in Georgia, a house is typically set back as much as 80 feet from the front of the property line; in California, a Spanish influence often appears both in design and planting; in Wisconsin, front yard design must take into account the destructive winter splashing of salt applied to icy roads; in Arizona, a compromise must be made between the need for shade and the necessity for openness in design to permit breezes to circulate.

Realize, also, that often extreme variation in climate from region to region causes designs that might appear to require high maintenance in your area actually to be low maintenance plantings in another region.

In examining this potpourri of design ideas, be aware that a considerable amount of oversimplification has been necessary in order to reduce a landscape architect's drawing to the printed page. Before you begin to redesign your property for low maintenance, you will benefit from seeking a landscape architect's professional help about such important considerations as drainage, city building codes, grading, plumbing, and wiring.

With *Sunset's* West as a base, this chapter radiates out to far corners of the country—from Oregon to New York, from California to Florida. On the facing page are listed the names of the professional men and women who have contributed so creatively to the diversity of ideas you'll see as you turn the pages.

CONTRIBUTING EXPERTS

R. David Adams, Landscape Designer, Seattle, Washington.

Theodore Brickman Company, Long Grove, Illinois. Theodore (Dick) Brickman, Landscape Architect. Mark B. Hunner, Landscape Architect.

Naud Burnett Associates, Dallas, Texas. Naud Burnett II, Landscape Architect, A.I.L.A. Richard Arthur, Landscape Architect, A.I.L.A. Albert T. David, Landscape Architect, A.I.L.A.

A. Gregory Catlow, Landscape Architect, Houston, Texas.

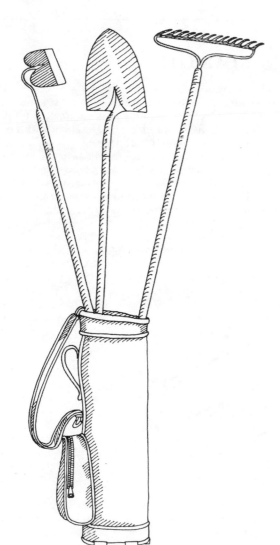

Glenn Cook, Landscape Architect, A.S.L.A., San Antonio, Texas.

B. G. Cunningham & Associates, Atlanta, Georgia. Barbara Cunningham, Environmental Planner.

Edward L. Daugherty, Landscape Architect, Atlanta, Georgia.

Chandler D. Fairbank, Landscape Architect, A.S.L.A., Portland, Oregon.

Todd Fry, Landscape Architect, San Diego, California.

Isabelle Greene Haller, Landscape Consultant, Santa Barbara, California.

Atlantic Nursery & Garden Shop, Freeport, New York. Rudi Harbauer, Landscape Designer.

Glen Hunt/Jerald Bell and Associates, Seattle, Washington. Glen Hunt, Landscape Architect.

Henry M. Lambert & Associates, Dallas, Texas. Erika Farkac, Landscape Architect.

Lied's Nursery Company, Inc., Sussex, Wisconsin. Thomas O. Lied, Landscape Architect. Patricia Davis, Landscape Architect. Donald Seamans, Landscape Architect.

F. J. MacDonald & Associates, Landscape Architects, Scottsdale, Arizona.

Chris G. Moritz, Inc., Denver, Colorado. Chris G. Moritz, Landscape Architect. David A. Younger, Landscape Designer.

Courtland Paul/Arthur Beggs and Associates, Pasadena, California. Courtland Paul, Landscape Architect. Arthur G. Beggs, Landscape Architect. Dennis Anderson, Landscape Architect.

Jo Ray, Landscape Architect and Site Planner. Eloise A. Ray, Landscape Architect and Associate. Westport, Connecticut.

E. Alan Rollinger, Landscape Designer, Broomfield, Colorado.

Roy Rydell, Landscape Architect, A.S.L.A., Santa Cruz, California.

Los Patios, Inc., San Antonio, Texas. John O. Spice, Landscape Architect.

W.E.D. Walt Disney World, Lake Buena Vista, Florida. Herbert Ramsaier, Landscape Designer. Scott Girard, Landscape Designer.

Chaffee-Zumwalt & Associates, Tacoma, Washington. A. Rex Zumwalt, Landscape Architect. Heidi Vukonich, Landscape Designer.

A Garden Fundamental: the Shape of your Lot

Homesites — like people — come in many shapes and sizes. And each shape and size presents its own challenge to the architect, contractor, landscape architect, and home gardener.

Quite often, home gardeners feel that their landscaping options are sharply narrowed by the shape of the lot they live on. But with a basic knowledge of garden design — and a creative assist from an experienced landscape architect — wonders of transformation can occur on even the plainest piece of property. Earth can rise and dip; water can flow; land that is exposed to the public can be reclaimed as a private enclave — even as garden maintenance is reduced from maximum to minimum.

Because a rectangular lot is one of the most common shapes, we've turned our attention to it first. At the bottom of this page is a familiar plan — a rectangular house, with driveway and garage in front and with entry, kitchen, living, dining, bedroom, and bath areas indicated. The house is set toward the front of a rectangular 75 by 125-foot lot.

Given this raw material to work from, what can a landscape architect do to create visual excitement, variety, and enduring living pleasure, at the same time keeping garden chores within reasonable bounds? Ten designers each provide different answers to this question on the next several pages.

TYPICAL RECTANGULAR LOT

Faced with some of the challenges of landscaping irregularly shaped lots, you may think, "Why didn't I just get a simple, flat rectangle of land to place my house upon?" On the other hand, when you look along a typical subdivision street of monotonous flat lots, you realize that there are challenges to be met there, as well.

How do you plant a typical rectangular lot in an interesting way, keeping in mind that you have no intention of spending your every waking hour taking care of it? First, think of the functions of each area and the relationship of the functions to those of the interior of the house. An exterior entrance area must accommodate vehicles as well as people. You need areas of utility that relate to the functions of garage, kitchen, and the maintenance of the garden itself.

Think about setting aside an area near the kitchen and dining room for outdoor eating, perhaps extending this to include room for further socializing, play, and lounging. From inside the house, you want to look out onto a series of attractive views.

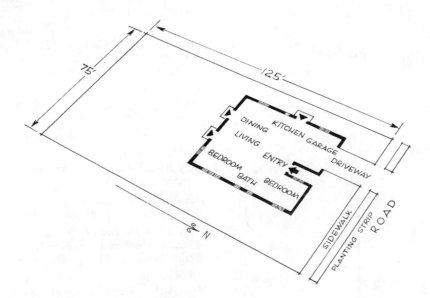

WITH ONE EXCEPTION, *the 10 landscape plans for typical lots that follow are based on the above sketch: a rectangular house placed on a 75 by 125-foot lot. The exception is the design for Atlanta, Georgia, where a house is often set back on a lot much more deeply than the one shown above.*

Palo Alto, California

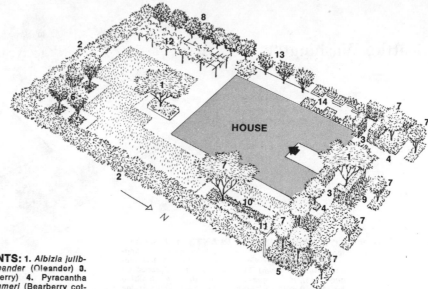

LOW MAINTENANCE PLANTS: 1. *Albizia julibrissin* (Silk tree) **2.** *Nerium oleander* (Oleander) **3.** *Prunus ilicifolia* (Hollyleaf cherry) **4.** Pyracantha 'Santa Cruz' **5.** *Cotoneaster dammeri* (Bearberry cotoneaster) **6.** *Prunus* 'Krauter Vesuvius' (Purple-leaf flowering plum) **7.** *Pittosporum undulatum* (Victorian box) **8.** Citrus **9.** *Agapanthus* (Lily-of-the-Nile) **10.** *Trachelospermum jasminoides* (Star jasmine) **11.** *Euryops pectinatus* **12.** Grape arbor **13.** Dwarf fruit trees **14.** Vegetable garden.

Design approach: Though the front garden is a minimum one, it offers a welcoming entry that is private from the street and permits access to both sides of the house. Ground covers, shrubs, and trees are plants that will take neglect once established but give color and interest all year. On the sunny, west side of the house, a neat but hidden utility area has room for vegetables and fruit. The remaining area is devoted to a pleasure garden with a lawn in the center surrounded by paving. Oleander as the background rarely needs attention but explodes with white blossoms for a good part of the summer. Trees add to the seasonal show and provide shade in specific areas. A patio under a grape arbor creates a spot for outdoor dining in the shade. This and a raised bed around the silk tree combat the flat look. Shade-loving annuals, such as impatiens, could be planted in the raised bed—or a shade-loving ground cover, such as ajuga, for the lowest maintenance. (Designed by Roy Rydell)

Pasadena, California

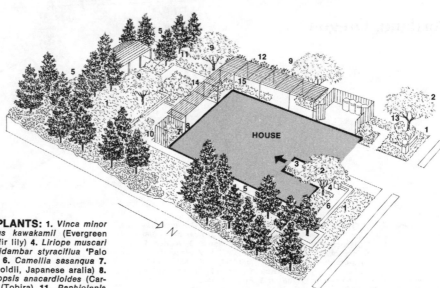

LOW MAINTENANCE PLANTS: 1. *Vinca minor* (Dwarf periwinkle) **2.** *Pyrus kawakamii* (Evergreen pear) **3.** *Clivia miniata* (Kaffir lily) **4.** *Liriope muscari* (Big blue lily turf) **5.** *Liquidambar styraciflua* 'Palo Alto' (American sweetgum) **6.** *Camellia sasanqua* **7.** *Fatsia japonica* (Aralia sieboldii, Japanese aralia) **8.** *Asplenium bulbiferum* (Mother fern) **9.** *Cupaniopsis anacardioides* (Carrot wood, Tuckeroo) **10.** *Pittosporum tobira* (Tobira) **11.** *Raphiolepis indica* 'Enchantress' (India hawthorn) **12.** Dwarf citrus trees **13.** *Ilex cornuta* 'Burfordii Nana' (Dwarf Burford holly) **14.** *Nandina domestica* 'Nana Compacta' (Dwarf heavenly bamboo) **15.** Mahonia aquifolium 'Nana' (Dwarf Oregon grape).

Design approach: Located at the edge of a canyon, this view lot has an up slope on one side. A continuous paved surface surrounds the house with a sizable expanse at the front entry and at the rear. A wooden trellis on the west side off the kitchen area provides sun control through mid-afternoon. A garden shelter and wooden deck for relaxing and viewing the city lights below are tucked behind carrotwood trees. Liquidambars clustered on the side slope and in the rear add to a sense of separation from neighbors. Most of the plants were selected for their moderate growth rate and require very little pruning. (Designed by Arthur G. Beggs)

Seattle, Washington

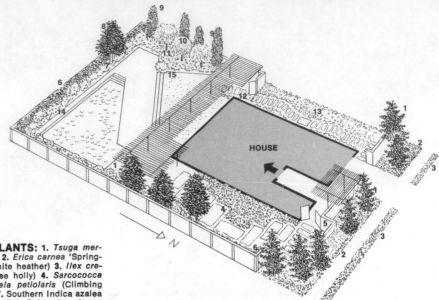

LOW MAINTENANCE PLANTS: 1. *Tsuga mertensiana* (Mountain hemlock) **2.** *Erica carnea* 'Springwood White' (Springwood white heather) **3.** *Ilex crenata* 'Helleri' (Dwarf Japanese holly) **4.** *Sarcococca humilis* **5.** *Hydrangea anomela petiolaris* (Climbing hydrangea) **6.** *Ilex ilicifolius* **7.** Southern Indica azalea 'Hino-crimson' **8.** *Prunus lusitanica* (Portugal laurel) **9.** *Calocedrus decurrens* (Incense cedar) **10.** *Prunus subhirtella autumnalis* (Autumn flowering cherry) **11.** *Daphne odora* **12.** *Pachysandra terminalis* (Japanese spurge) **13.** Rhododendron 'Decorum' **14.** Annuals, bulbs **15.** Containers for seasonal color.

Design approach: Faced with a flat lot on which sits a contemporary flat-roofed house with much glass on two sides, the designer decided on a grade change to create the illusion of space. He arranged for a change of contour in two ways: 1) in front, a *visual* change only, created by a one-sided berm that is backed by a concrete wall, creating an inner courtyard leading to the pool; 2) an *actual* grade change in back, where the swimming pool and deck area are set down 18 inches and surrounded by a 24-inch retaining wall to hold up original property grade. Low maintenance points: no lawn at all; no monthly upkeep of any planting area. Trees are placed far from the pool to help keep the water free from litter. Heather on the berm needs once-a-year care after blooming. (Designed by R. David Adams)

Portland, Oregon

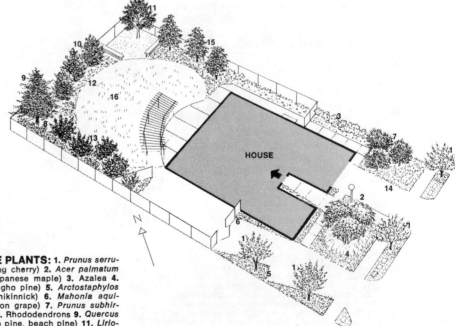

LOW MAINTENANCE PLANTS: 1. *Prunus serrulata* 'Sekiyama' (Flowering cherry) **2.** *Acer palmatum* 'Dissectum' (Laceleaf Japanese maple) **3.** Azalea **4.** *Pinus mugo mughus* (Mugho pine) **5.** *Arctostaphylos uva-ursi* (Bearberry, Kinnikinnick) **6.** *Mahonia aquifolium* 'Compacta' (Oregon grape) **7.** *Prunus subhirtella autumnalis* (Autumn flowering cherry) **8.** Rhododendrons **9.** *Quercus palustris* (Pin oak) **10.** *Pinus contorta* (Shore pine, beach pine) **11.** *Liriodendron tulipifera* (Tulip tree) **12.** Annuals or low vegetables **13.** *Cornus nuttallii* (Pacific dogwood) **14.** *Cotoneaster horizontalis* (Rock cotoneaster) **15.** *Liquidambar styraciflua* (American sweetgum) **16.** Lawn.

Design approach: The owners of this home like to garden but also like to be able to leave their garden without having it grow into a state of rack and ruin. Pines, oaks, and shrubs provide minimum-care, year-round vegetation; flowering cherry, dogwood, and the Japanese maple provide color at various times. The tulip tree was planted in the play area for children's climbing, as well as for its flowers. A separate area for annuals or vegetables can be worked in or not, as the owners choose. Crushed rock on the wider side yard offers enclosed boat storage. The path on the other side of the house follows a dry stream bed. Trees around the perimeter of the rear garden and the arbor give privacy to the patio. (Designed by Chandler D. Fairbank)

San Antonio, Texas

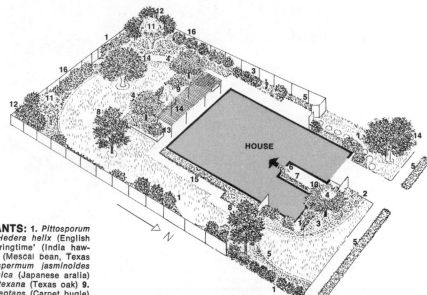

LOW MAINTENANCE PLANTS: 1. *Pittosporum tobira* 'Variegata' (Tobira) **2.** *Hedera helix* (English ivy) **3.** *Raphiolepis indica* 'Springtime' (India hawthorn) **4.** *Sophora secundiflora* (Mescal bean, Texas mountain laurel) **5.** *Trachelospermum jasminoides* (Star jasmine) **6.** *Fatsia japonica* (Japanese aralia) **7.** *Aspidistra elatior* (Cast-iron plant) **8.** *Quercus texana* (Texas oak) **9.** *Ophiopogon japonicus* (Mondo grass) **10.** *Ajuga reptans* (Carpet bugle) **11.** *Eriobotrya japonica* (Loquat) **12.** *Lagerstroemia indica* 'Petite' (Dwarf crape myrtle) **13.** *Rosmarinus officinalis* 'Prostratus' (Dwarf rosemary) **14.** *Quercus virginiana* (Southern live oak) **15.** Cut flowers: roses and annuals **16.** *Photinia fraseri.*

Design approach: Plants in this landscape grow easily in the hot, dry summers and alkaline soil and water of southern Texas. Trees, lattice or roofed terrace, and entry areas provide shade. Raised beds encourage healthy growth by providing deeper, richer soil and expand outdoor living space with seating around patio areas. A gently curving lawn perimeter allows easy mowing. Ground covers replace lawn in small, hard-to-mow areas. Containers in the entry and patio areas can provide quick splashes of color when the owners have the time to care for the tubbed plantings. (Designed by John O. Spice)

Houston, Texas

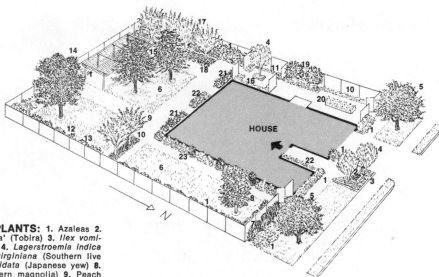

LOW MAINTENANCE PLANTS: 1. Azaleas **2.** *Pittosporum tobira* 'Variegata' (Tobira) **3.** *Ilex vomitoria* 'Nana' (Dwarf yaupon) **4.** *Lagerstroemia indica* (Crape myrtle) **5.** *Quercus virginiana* (Southern live oak) **6.** Lawn **7.** *Taxus cuspidata* (Japanese yew) **8.** *Magnolia grandiflora* (Southern magnolia) **9.** Peach trees **10.** *Liriope muscari* (Big blue lily turf) **11.** *Ligustrum japonicum* (Japanese privet) **12.** *Camellia japonica* **13.** *Ajuga reptans* (Carpet bugle) **14.** *Quercus rubra* (Red oak) **15.** *Quercus nigra* (Water oak) **16.** *Trachelospermum jasminoides* (Star jasmine) **17.** White flowering peach trees **18.** *Asparagus densiflorus* 'Sprengeri' (Sprenger asparagus) **19.** *Eriobotrya japonica* (Loquat trees) **20.** Annuals **21.** *Nandina domestica* 'Nana' (Dwarf heavenly bamboo) **22.** *Moraea iridioides* (Evergreen iris) **23.** *Raphiolepis indica* (India hawthorn).

Design approach: Most of this lot is planted in evergreen materials that add bloom, shape, and texture to the garden without requiring much attention. The only high maintenance elements are the lawn, which is placed within masonry borders to facilitate edging, and the seasonal planting bed, which was kept small. Different varieties of azaleas offer a long blooming season and only require annual feeding and pruning. The Japanese privet and India hawthorn require no pruning. Flowering fruit trees produce showy blossoms with little attention. Ajuga acts as a ground cover under the camellias. (Designed by A. Gregory Catlow)

Denver, Colorado

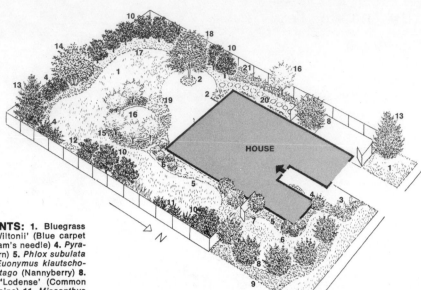

LOW MAINTENANCE PLANTS: 1. Bluegrass lawn **2.** *Juniperus horizontalis* 'Wiltonii' (Blue carpet juniper) **3.** *Yucca filamentosa* (Adam's needle) **4.** *Pyracantha coccinea* 'Wyatti' (Firethorn) **5.** *Phlox subulata* (Moss pink, Creeping phlox) **6.** *Euonymus kiautschovica* 'Manhattan' **7.** *Viburnum lentago* (Nannyberry) **8.** *Acer ginnala* (Amur maple) **9.** *Ligustrum vulgare* 'Lodense' (Common privet) **10.** *Pinus cembroides edulis* (Mexican pinon pine) **11.** *Miscanthus sinensis* (Eulalia grass) **12.** *Potentilla* (Cinquefoil) **13.** *Pinus nigra* (Austrian black pine) **14.** *Betula nigra* (River birch) **15.** *Juniperus horizontalis* (Prostrata juniper) **16.** *Malus* 'Flame' (crabapple) **17.** *Symphoricarpos chenaultii* 'Hancock' **18.** *Gleditsia triacanthos inermis* 'Skyline' (Honey locust) **19.** Annuals **20.** Herbs **21.** Raspberries.

Design approach: The plant material here, selected for the high plains area, can be allowed to grow naturally with little pruning and shaping. This gives the garden an informal, natural look, in addition to minimizing upkeep. A 3-inch layer

of crushed rock placed over black polyethylene retains soil moisture and controls weed growth. Low, spreading shrubs will cover most of this area in time. A steel strap was used as edging to keep lawn from invading planting areas and to maintain the curving lines of the garden. (Designed by Chris G. Moritz)

Chicago, Illinois

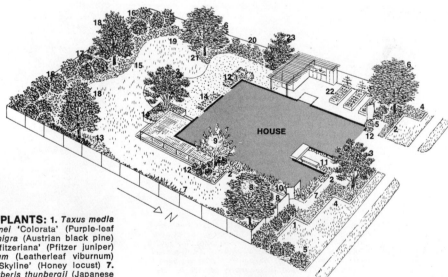

LOW MAINTENANCE PLANTS: 1. *Taxus media* (Yew) **2.** *Euonymus fortunei* 'Colorata' (Purple-leaf winter creeper) **3.** *Pinus nigra* (Austrian black pine) **4.** *Juniperus chinensis* 'Pfitzeriana' (Pfitzer juniper) **5.** *Viburnum rhytidophyllum* (Leatherleaf viburnum) **6.** *Gleditsia triacanthos* 'Skyline' (Honey locust) **7.** *Forsythia intermedia* (Border forsythia) **8.** *Berberis thunbergii* (Japanese barberry) **9.** *Cercis canadensis* (Eastern redbud) **10.** *Forsythia viridissima* 'Bronxensis' **11.** Rhododendron **12.** *Euonymus fortunei* 'Sarcoxie' **13.** Annuals **14.** *Juniperus procumbens* (Japanese garden juniper) **15.** *Cotoneaster apiculata* (Cranberry cotoneaster) **16.** *Viburnum dentatum* (Arrowwood) **17.** *Cornus alba* 'Sibirica' (Dogwood) **18.** *Acer rubrum* (Scarlet maple) **19.** *Potentilla* (Cinquefoil) **20.** *Rhus typhina* (Staghorn sumac) **21.** *Cotoneaster divaricata* (Spreading cotoneaster) **22.** Espaliered fruit trees and vegetables **23.** *Pinus banksiana* (Jack pine).

Design approach: Here the entry court has been designed to direct traffic around, instead of through, planting beds. An Austrian pine creates a natural canopy, and flowering

shrubs beneath add dependable greenery and color. Purple-leaf winter creeper requires care at first but becomes a low maintenance filler once established. Lawn, used because of its low cost, is designed for minimum raking and trimming by placing most trees in shrub beds and by generous use of mowing strips. (Designed by Dick Brickman and Mark B. Hunner)

Atlanta, Georgia

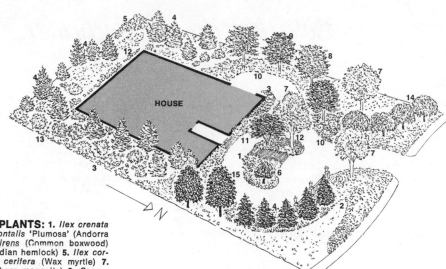

LOW MAINTENANCE PLANTS: 1. *Ilex crenata* 'Helleri' **2.** *Juniperus horizontalis* 'Plumosa' (Andorra juniper) **3.** *Buxus sempervirens* (Common boxwood) **4.** *Tsuga canadensis* (Canadian hemlock) **5.** *Ilex cornuta* 'Burfordii' **6.** *Myrica cerifera* (Wax myrtle) **7.** *Magnolia grandiflora* (Southern magnolia) **8.** *Cornus florida* (Flowering dogwood) 'White Cloud' **9.** *Cornus florida* 'Spring Song' **10.** *Hedera helix* (English ivy) **11.** *Acer palmatum* (Japanese maple) **12.** *Kurume azaleas* 'Coral bell' **13.** Rhododendrons **14.** *Prunus subhirtella pendula* (Single weeping cherry) **15.** *Pinus canariensis* (Canary Island pine).

Design approach: Like many lots in Atlanta, this one occupies a full acre. In the traditional southern manner, the house is set back 80 or more feet, creating an exceptionally deep front lawn. To eliminate the high upkeep of this lawn, the drive was arranged to break up the area into manageable sections, while still providing a graceful design. The magnolia, dogwood, and weeping cherry trees flower abundantly; additional bloom comes from the azaleas and rhododendrons. Most of these plants require annual feeding, pruning, and some summer watering. Upkeep beyond that is minimal because tree litter falls into the shrubs and ivy. Varieties were selected that maintain their naturally good shapes without pruning. Expansive walkways cut down on the amount of planting. (Designed by Barbara Cunningham)

Orlando, Florida

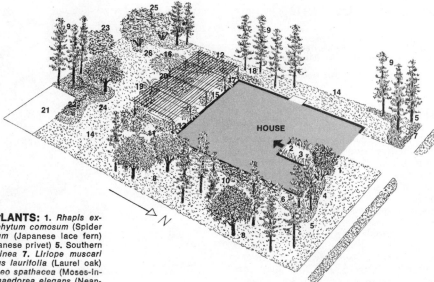

LOW MAINTENANCE PLANTS: 1. *Rhapis excelsa* (Lady palm) **2.** *Chlorophytum comosum* (Spider plant) **3.** *Polystichum setosum* (Japanese lace fern) **4.** *Ligustrum japonicum* (Japanese privet) **5.** Southern indica azalea **6.** *Ixora coccinea* **7.** *Liriope muscari* (Big blue lily turf) **8.** *Quercus laurifolia* (Laurel oak) **9.** Existing pines **10.** *Gardenia* 'Veitchii' **11.** *Rhoeo spathacea* (Moses-in-the-cradle) **12.** *Begonia semperflorens* **13.** *Chamaedorea elegans* (Neanthe bella, parlor palm) **14.** Argentine bahia grass **15.** *Camellia sasanqua* **16.** *Peltophorum dubium* **17.** *Dracaena marginata* **18.** *Ilex cornuta* 'Burfordii' **19.** *Cycas revoluta* (Sago palm) **20.** *Severina buxifolia* **21.** Vegetable and cutting garden **22.** *Wedelia trilobata* **23.** *Bauhinia galpinii* (Red bauhinia) **24.** *Gardenia jasminoides* **25.** *Franklinia alatamaha* **26.** *Thryallis glauca*.

Design approach: Trees provide shade in this tropical garden; a cypress mulch under them keeps down weeds. Existing trees that thrived on the lot—such as the oaks and pines —were left in place and new, low maintenance plantings worked in around them. To eliminate weeds that are a continual problem in a lush environment, shrubs are massed, and such ground covers as liriope and wedelia fill any bare spots. Flowering shrubs (azalea, gardenia, and camellia) provide seasonal color. (Designed by Herbert Ramsaier)

Lots that Present Particular Problems

Suppose that your lot is *not* rectangular. Yours may then be a challenge not to add zest to predictable property but rather to control the demands of an expansive corner lot or to tame a runaway slope.

How your lot is shaped will probably have a considerable effect on your home lifestyle. For example, a corner lot will give you a maximum of public exposure and often a minimum of private garden area. A pie-shaped lot, on the other hand, tends to reverse this situation. If you are landscaping a hillside lot, you may have to hang your garden on a hill in order to surround yourself with greenery at all.

In this section, we've asked designers to confront low maintenance landscaping problems that really require an imaginative leap to cope with. First, the corner lot is dealt with for gardens in California, Texas, Georgia, Illinois, and Colorado. Then four other irregular or problem lots are presented: the deep, narrow urban lot; the pie-shaped lot; the hillside lot; and the town house lot with small gardens.

Remember that, wherever you live, you can adapt design elements from anywhere in the country to improve your garden and make it easier to tend. So study over all of the designs for ideas that appeal to you.

CORNER LOT

Seen from two sides, a corner lot has a greater responsibility to the public eye than any other type of lot. How to contribute to your neighborhood without spending a lifetime manicuring plants that are rarely within your view is the major challenge here.

From examining the super-abundant streetside exposure on the plans that follow, you'll conclude that ground covers (alive or inanimate) can be your ally. This is an area where you will possibly consider eliminating the maintenance-demanding lawn. And this type of property location may also cause you to get some of this public space back into your private domain. Depending upon your local civic site restrictions, this can sometimes be accomplished with the aid of trees and fences or hedges.

Carmel, California

LOW MAINTENANCE PLANTS: 1. *Eucalyptus polyanthemos* (Silver dollar gum) **2.** *Malus floribunda* (Japanese flowering crabapple) **3.** *Pittosporum undulatum* **4.** *Juniperus horizontalis* 'Wiltonii' (Blue carpet juniper) **5.** *Raphiolepis indica* (India hawthorn) **6.** *Rhamnus alaternus* (Italian buckthorn) **7.** *Citrus* **8.** *Cornus florida* (Flowering dogwood) **9.** *Sarcococca ruscifolia.*

Design approach: A circular driveway makes a spacious entry and provides additional parking. This allows a very simple streetside planting with the street trees incorporated into the total design. Color is provided here by the flowering crabapple and raphiolepis, making frequent disturbing and replanting of beds unnecessary. The raphiolepis also stays compact and well-shaped without pruning. A screened area off the kitchen and a service area by the garage take care of equipment, garbage disposal, and other service needs. The private part of the garden has a terrace at floor level convenient for lounging and for alfresco dining. This terrace looks down on a small but interestingly shaped lawn that has no interruptions requiring hand clipping. A concealed spot in the sun can be used for vegetables and cut flowers or can be neglected and still not detract from the rest of the garden. (Designed by Roy Rydell)

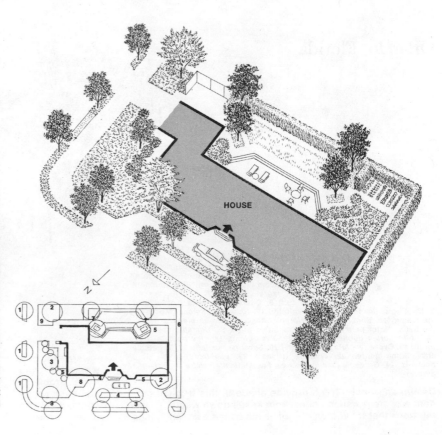

Atlanta, Georgia

LOW MAINTENANCE PLANTS: 1. *Cornus florida alba* (White dogwood) **2.** *Hedera helix* (English ivy) **3.** Lawn **4.** *Cercis* (Redbuds) **5.** *Ilex cornuta* 'Burfordii' (Burford holly) **6.** *Magnolia grandiflora* (Southern magnolia) **7.** *Hemerocallis* (Daylily) **8.** Southern indica azalea **9.** Kurume azalea **10.** Southern indica azalea 'Flame Creeper' **11.** *Mahonia bealei* (Leatherleaf mahonia) **12.** *Tsuga canadensis* (Canada hemlock) **13.** *Quercus virginiana* (Southern live oak) **14.** *Nandina domestica* (Heavenly bamboo) **15.** *Lagerstroemia indica* (Crape myrtle) **16.** *Ilex crenata* 'Convexa' (Convex-leaf Japanese holly) **17.** *Ilex vomitoria* (Yaupon) **18.** *Prunus caroliniana* (Carolina laurel cherry).

Design approach: An ivy ground cover in front confines the lawn to a manageable area and catches leaf fall from the dogwood trees. Flagstone paves the entry walk. Screens and plantings near the rear of the house set off a service yard from the brick patio. From this secluded patio, the owners can enjoy the bloom of the magnolias and shade and privacy from the Canadian hemlocks. Flame azaleas burst into color under the oaks in the spring. The massed mahonia produces a striking winter picture with its bronzy foliage. (Designed by Edward L. Daugherty)

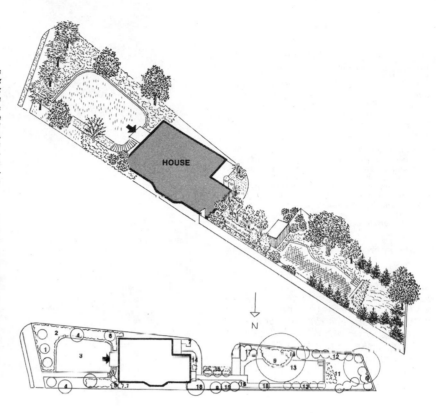

Denver, Colorado

LOW MAINTENANCE PLANTS: 1. *Yucca filamentosa* (Adam's needle) **2.** *Juniperus horizontalis* 'Wiltonii' (Blue carpet juniper) **3.** *Juniperus sabina* 'Buffalo' **4.** *Euonymus kiautschovica* 'Manhattan' **5.** *Gleditsia triacanthos* 'Skyline' (Honey locust) **6.** *Mahonia aquifolium* (Oregon grape) **7.** *Pyracantha coccinea* 'Pauciflora' (Scarlet firethorn) **8.** *Cotoneaster apiculata* (Cranberry cotoneaster) **9.** *Populus tremuloides* (Quaking aspen) **10.** *Euonymus fortunei* 'Colorata' (Purple-leaf winter creeper) **11.** *Pinus sylvestris* (Scotch pine) **12.** *Pyracantha coccinea* 'Wyattii' (Firethorn) **13.** *Berberis mentorensis* (Mentor barberry) **14.** *Juniperus sabina* 'Tamariscifolia' (Tamarix juniper) **15.** *Malus ioensis plena* (Bechtel crabapple) **16.** *Rhus glabra* (Smooth sumac) **17.** *Miscanthus sinensis* (Eulalia, Plume grass).

Design approach: Giving unity to this design is the brick and wood theme. Railroad ties installed flush with the lawn serve as a mowing strip, assuring greater ease in lawn care, and the ties are also used among the brick of the patio and entrance walk. At least 2-inch-thick bark mulch covers planting beds to retain moisture, discourage weed growth, and carry out the wood theme. Color among the evergreen pines, junipers, and shrubs appears seasonally on the pyracantha, cotoneaster, and the row of crabapple trees. (Designed by Chris G. Moritz)

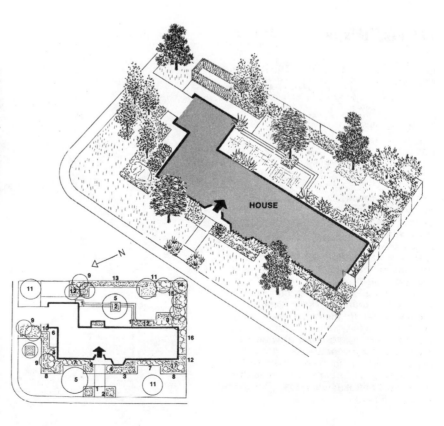

Chicago, Illinois

LOW MAINTENANCE PLANTS: 1. *Fraxinus pennsylvanica* 'Marshall' (Marshall seedless green ash) 2. *Gleditsia triacanthos* 'Skyline' (Honey locust) 3. *Euonymus fortunei* 'Colorata' (Purple-leaf winter creeper) 4. *Thuja occidentalis* (American arborvitae) 5. Rhododendrons 6. *Pinus nigra* (Austrian black pine) 7. *Berberis thunbergii* (Japanese barberry) 8. *Juniperus chinensis* 'Pfitzeriana Nana' (Dwarf Pfitzer juniper) 9. *Euonymus fortunei radicans* 'Sarcoxie' 10. *Pinus mugo mughus* (Mugho pine) 11. *Euonymus erecta* 12. Yucca 13. *Cercis canadensis* (Eastern redbud) 14. *Pyrus calleryana* (Ornamental pear) 15. Espaliered fruit trees 16. *Potentilla* 'Katherine Dykes' 17. *Hedera helix gracilis* (English ivy) 18. *Pinus banksiana* (Jack pine) 19. *Elaeagnus angustifolia* (Russian olive) 20. *Cotoneaster apiculata* (Cranberry cotoneaster) 21. *Viburnum rhytidophyllum* (Leatherleaf viburnum) 22. *Cornus baileyi* (Dogwood).

Design approach: The tightness of the site suggested the vertical materials of arborvitae hedges and redwood fences for screening and defining garden areas. Most trees are planted in shrub beds to minimize leaf removal. Plants native to the area are emphasized both for natural looks and for lower upkeep. (Designed by Dick Brickman and Mark B. Hunner)

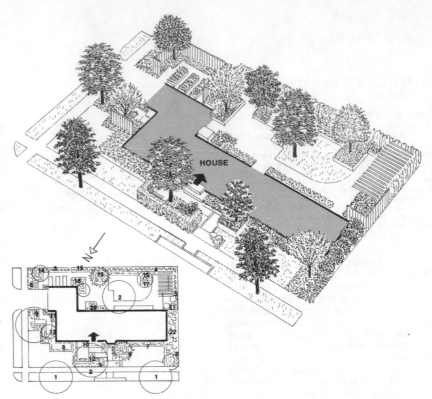

Dallas, Texas

LOW MAINTENANCE PLANTS: 1. St. Augustine grass 2. Kurume azaleas 3. *Buxus microphylla japonica* (Japanese boxwood) 4. *Quercus rubra* (Red oak) 5. *Ophiopogon japonicum* (Mondo grass) 6. Herb garden 7. *Camellia sasanqua* 'White Dove' 8. *Ilex cornuta* 'Burfordii' (Burford holly) 9. *Quercus virginiana* (Southern live oak) 10. *Gelesmium sempervirens* (Carolina jessamine) 11. *Liriope muscari* 'Silvery Sunproof' (Big blue lily turf) 12. *Ajuga reptans* (Carpet bugle) 13. *Raphiolepis indica* (India hawthorn) 14. *Trachelospermum asiaticum* (Asiatic star jasmine).

Design approach: Oval pools and brick paving give this garden a formal look without the maintenance usually associated with a formal garden. Loose form plants are emphasized—azaleas, camellias, and raphiolepis, all needing little pruning and having a long bloom season. Although the boxwood is shaped, it is a slow-growing, compact plant, needing only yearly pruning. These evergreens, along with the liriope, ophiopogon, ajuga, and star jasmine ground covers and the evergreen oaks and lawn, provide year-round greenery, punctuated by the bloom of the flowering shrubs. The tall Burford holly and the Carolina jessamine hide equipment and service yards. (Designed by Erika Farkac)

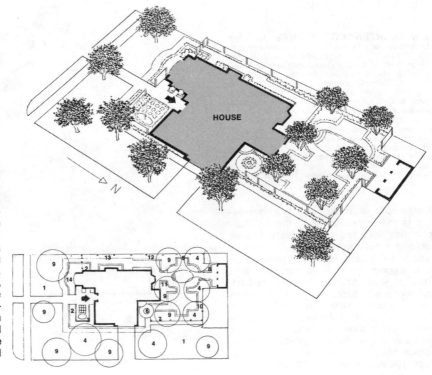

DEEP, NARROW URBAN LOT

Most old cities and a number of new communities were laid out with a minimum of street frontage for a maximum of square footage of property. In some cases, homes have side yards only wide enough to push a wheelbarrow through. But often, materials needed in the rear must be carted through the house or basement.

Without four sides to develop, you have two exposures in which to plant your low maintenance garden. You're fortunate if you have a south garden in this situation. You can create shade where you want it, and you can welcome the winter sun into the private part of your dwelling. If not, ingenuity is called for, and you may find yourself considering space in new terms. Perhaps you will begin to think of second floor decks to get you and your herbage closer to the sun. Possibly, you will consider building a bridge to a shelter beyond. Select plants that will live in this environment and take its limitations in their stride. Look for lifeless materials, such as brick, to add warmth to a wall or floor where nothing will grow.

San Francisco, California

LOW MAINTENANCE PLANTS: 1. *Pittosporum crassifolium* **2.** *Laurus nobilis* (Sweet bay, Grecian laurel) **3.** *Malus* 'Hopa' (Flowering crabapple) **4.** *Trachelospermum jasminoides* (Star jasmine) **5.** *Raphiolepis indica* (India hawthorn) **6.** *Juniperus conferta* (Shore juniper) **7.** *Camellia japonica* **8.** *Magnolia grandiflora* (Southern magnolia) **9.** *Hebe* 'Patty's purple' **10.** Bulbs, annuals **11.** *Prunus cerasifera* 'Krauter Vesuvius.'

Design approach: The tiny entrance from a busy city street gains a measure of privacy from a wall with gates and small trees that screen traffic and help reduce noise. Flagstone used for paving offers a warm contrast to the cold sidewalk. The rear garden gives an illusion of greater space than really exists because the plant materials are massed. This garden provides more than one area where a chair can be moved to follow the sun. Background shrubs are kept simple so the small garden does not look too busy. Trees give the garden a roof and burst into spectacular bloom in season. Spots among the shrubs and trees are left free for a few bulbs and annuals, but these are not necessary because the trees and shrubs provide year-round color and interest. Once the plantings are established, maintenance is reduced to summer watering, not much of a problem in the cool climate of this city. (Designed by Roy Rydell)

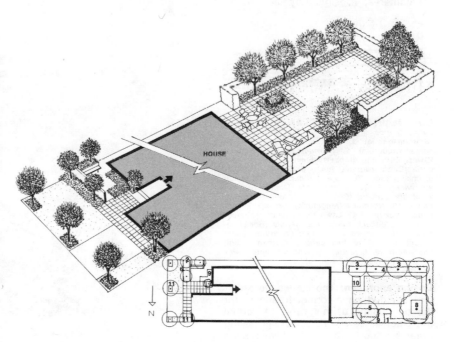

Seattle, Washington

LOW MAINTENANCE PLANTS: 1. *Hedera helix* 'Hahn's self branching' **2.** *Pinus thunbergiana* (Japanese black pine) **3.** *Viburnum davidii* **4.** *Nandina domestica* (Heavenly bamboo) **5.** Rhododendron **6.** *Hebe glaucophylla* **7.** *Sarcococca humilis* **8.** *Cornus mas* 'Nana' (Dwarf Cornelian cherry, dogwood) **9.** *Raphiolepis indica* 'Rosea' (Pink India hawthorn) **10.** *Acer circinatum* (Vine maple) **11.** *Ilex crenata* 'Convexa' (Japanese holly) **12.** *Betula verrucosa* 'Fastigata' (Pyramidal white birch) **13.** *Calluna vulgaris* 'Mrs. J. H. Hamilton' (Scotch heather) **14.** *Prunus sargentii* (Sargent cherry) **15.** *Potentilla* (Cinquefoil) **16.** *Pachysandra terminalis* (Japanese spurge) **17.** *Thymus lanuginosus* (Woolly thyme) **18.** *Senecio cineraria* (Dusty miller) **19.** *Pinus contorta* (Shore pine).

Design approach: A planting strip at streetside, paved with brick set in sand, leads to the front door. Privacy for the entry and a sitting area here are achieved with a 6-foot-high wooden screen. Both side yards are paved with finely crushed rock on a bed of sand. Stepping stones set in the rock lead around one side of the house. The rear garden is designed for outdoor living with areas planned for viewing from both outside and inside the house. A generous use of paving, rocks, and ground covers gives the design continuity and cuts down on maintenance. Flowering shrubs, such as viburnum, raphiolepis, and rhododendron, offer seasonal interest. (Designed by Glen Hunt)

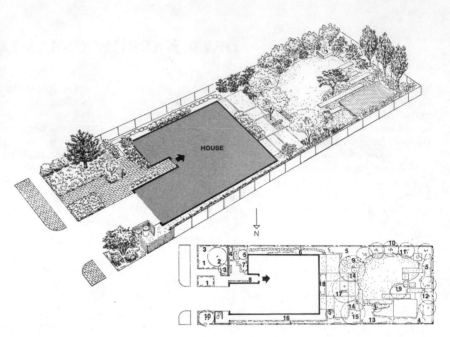

Milwaukee, Wisconsin

LOW MAINTENANCE PLANTS: 1. *Myrica pennsylvanica* (Bayberry) **2.** *Magnolia stellata* (Star magnolia) **3.** *Viburnum carlesii* (Korean spice virburnum) **4.** *Viburnum opulus* 'Nanum' (Dwarf European cranberry bush) **5.** *Kochia scoparia* 'Culta' (Burning bush) **6.** *Syringa vulgaris* (Common lilac) **7.** *Thuja occidentalis* (American arborvitae) **8.** *Taxus cuspidata* (Japanese yew) **9.** *Malus baccata* 'Columnaris' (Columnar crabapple) **10.** *Rhamnus frangula* 'Columnaris' (Tallhedge buckthorn) **11.** Lawn **12.** *Potentilla* (Cinquefoil) **13.** *Gleditsia triacanthos inermis* (Honey locust) **14.** *Hydrangea arborescens grandiflora* (Hills of Snow) **15.** *Tilia americana* (American linden, basswood) **16.** *Ligustrum* (Privet) **17.** *Betula verrucosa* (European white birch).

Design approach: The landscape architect decided on a formal treatment for the remodeling of this very old, formal brick home. New York bluestone paving creates a courtyard entry and widens the drive, assisting in winter snow removal and providing a walkway from the rear garage area to the front entry. A large piece of sculpture creates a focal point in the rear garden. Arborvitae on either end screen out neighboring houses and give winter color. Plants, such as the viburnum and hydrangea, provide color throughout the year without the need for seasonal plantings that require greater care. (Designed by Donald Seamans)

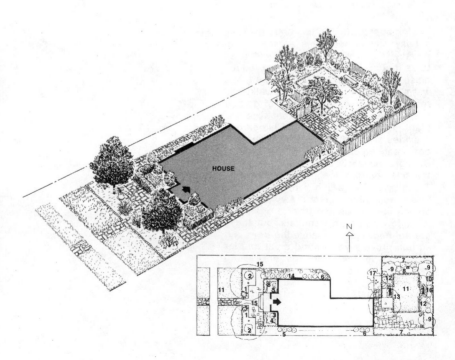

Dallas, Texas

LOW MAINTENANCE PLANTS: 1. *Ilex cornuta* 'Rotunda' (Dwarf Chinese holly) **2.** *Pittosporum tobira* (Tobira) **3.** *Photinia fraseri* **4.** *Quercus chrysolepis* (Canyon live oak) **5.** Wisteria **6.** Camellias **7.** Azaleas **8.** Vegetables and cutting flowers in raised beds. **9.** *Pinus thunbergiana* (Japanese black pine) **10.** *Cleyera japonica* **11.** *Trachelospermum asiaticum* (Yellow star jasmine) **12.** *Raphiolepis indica* 'Jack Evans' (India hawthorn) **13.** *Yucca recurvifolia* **14.** *Lagerstroemia indica* (Crape myrtle) **15.** *Ilex vomitoria* (Yaupon) **16.** *Aucuba japonica* 'Variegata' (Gold dust plant) **17.** *Ilex cornuta* 'Burfordii'.

Design approach: Working to utilize all existing space within the requirements of the building codes, the designer assured low maintenance by eliminating all grass and using ground covers and shrubs. Because his clients wanted a natural setting in an urban environment, he concentrated on soft plantings in the rear garden, random placement of shrubs, a small pool stocked with koi, stone paths, a free-form terrace, and a wooden screen hiding the vegetable garden. A fountain is a decorative feature viewed from both inside and out. The inside greenhouse with translucent roof and tropical plants, visible from all rooms, is used for indoor/outdoor dining. The greenhouse gives natural light inside the house and creates a feeling of added space. Privacy is provided by planting screens and wall. (Designed by Naud Burnett Associates)

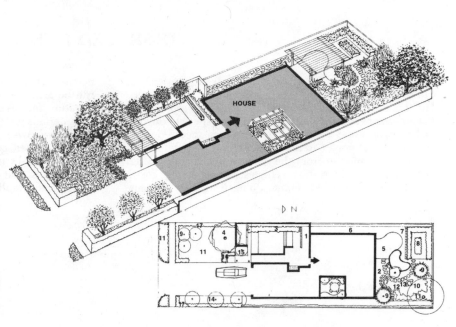

Freeport, New York

LOW MAINTENANCE PLANTS: 1. *Tsuga canadensis* (Canada hemlock) **2.** *Pyracantha coccinea* (Firethorn) **3.** *Pinus nigra* (Austrian black pine) **4.** *Cotoneaster horizontalis* (Rock cotoneaster) **5.** *Juniperus chinensis* 'Pfitzeriana' (Pfitzer juniper) **6.** *Acer palmatum* 'Atropurpureum' (Red Japanese maple) **7.** *Juniperus horizontalis* 'Wiltonii' (Blue carpet juniper) **8.** *Gleditsia triacanthos inermis* (Honey locust) **9.** *Ligustrum obtusifolium* (Border privet) **10.** *Ilex crenata* (Japanese holly) **11.** *Cornus florida* (Flowering dogwood) **12.** *Kalmia latifolia* (Mountain laurel) **13.** *Cryptomeria japonica* (Japanese cryptomeria) **14.** *Pieris japonica* (Lily-of-the-valley shrub) **15.** Lawn. **16.** *Pinus mugho mughus* (Mugho pine) **17.** *Photinia fraseri* **18.** Rhododendrons **19.** *Betula verrucosa* (European white birch) **20.** *Picea pungens* 'Glauca' (Colorado blue spruce **21.** Roses **22.** *Oxydendrum arboreum* (Sorrel tree).

Design approach. Owners of this home feel that time invested in pool and lawn maintenance is worth the recreation dividends, so the rest of the lot must be able to take care of itself. An expansive drive leading to the entrance and the wide wooden deck in the rear are convenient and reduce the amount of plant materials. Color, for the most part, comes from the permanent shrubs and trees. (Designed by Rudi Harbauer)

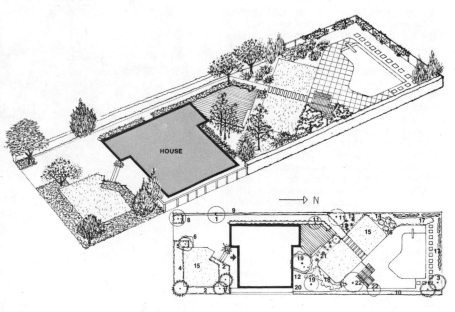

PIE-SHAPED LOT

Often the pie-shaped lot that is apt to front on a *cul de sac* offers the most for his money to the property owner. He has the absolute minimum frontage to keep up for his neighbors and the absolute maximum space to devote to his private use. Yet that space presents special design problems that need careful planning.

In that minimum front, he has the problem of taking care of his transportation vehicles and arranging for a suitable entrance to his home, doing it all in a gracious

manner. However, that comparatively vast rear garden can be arranged to suit his fancy. If he wants to return to nature and his climate allows, he can have a wilderness, a mysterious jungle. If he decides to turn it into a modest truck farm, who is to care? If the neighbors don't object, he might even consider a chicken or two. Wanting to keep the yard's maintenance at a minimum, he'll study the designs that follow in this section and find many ways of accomplishing his goals.

Santa Barbara, California

LOW MAINTENANCE PLANTS: 1. *Pinus halepensis* (Aleppo pine) **2.** *Heteromeles arbutifolia* (Toyon) **3.** *Psidium cattleianum* (Strawberry guava) **4.** *Raphiolepis indica* 'Enchantress' (India hawthorn) **5.** *Potentilla verna* (Spring cinquefoil) **6.** *Jacaranda acutifolia* **7.** *Arctostaphylos densiflora* 'Howard McMinn' (Vine hill manzanita) **8.** *Quercus agrifolia* (Coast live oak) **9.** *Juniperus chinensis* 'Pfitzeriana' (Pfitzer juniper) **10.** Lawn **11.** *Ilex altaclarensis* 'Wilsonii' (Wilson holly) **12.** *Coprosma repens* 'Variegata' (Mirror plant).

Design approach: On this lot, sloping downward to the rear with a level pad cut for the house and lower pad for a rear yard, only the cut land was planted. Existing oaks on the hillside provide shade and a leaf mulch to keep down weeds; those weeds that come through are mowed yearly. Plantings in the landscaped area were selected for minimum care and to blend with the surrounding woods. Most of the plants need only occasional summer watering. The manzanita was mulched with chipped tree trimmings to hold down weeds and conserve moisture; it needs no care once established. Packed, decomposed granite covers the ground between plants in the front garden and was installed after the area was sprayed with an herbicide. A sculpture and wall mural in the entry complements the planting there. The large deck in the rear invites the owners outdoors. (Designed by Isabelle Greene Haller)

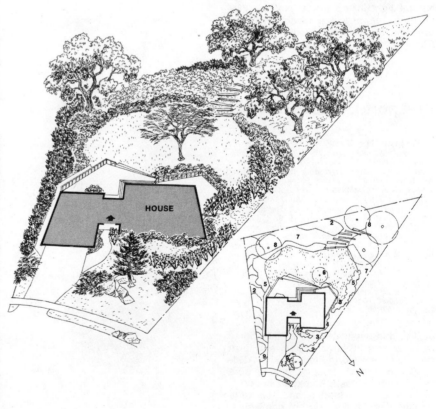

Tacoma, Washington

LOW MAINTENANCE PLANTS: 1. *Platanus acerfolia* (London plane tree) **2.** *Mahonia aquifolium* 'Compacta' (Dwarf Oregon grape) **3.** *Mahonia aquifolium* (Oregon grape) **4.** Rhododendrons **5.** *Mahonia nervosa* (Cascades mahonia) **6.** *Skimmia japonica* (Japanese skimmia) **7.** *Prunus subhirtella autumnalis* (Autumn flowering cherry) **8.** *Pieris japonica* (Japanese pieris) **9.** *Acer circinatum* (Vine maple) **10.** *Pinus contorta* (Shore pine) **11.** *Cornus nuttallii* (Pacific dogwood) **12.** *Tsuga heterophylla* (Western hemlock) **13.** *Photinia glabra* (Japanese photinia) **14.** *Vaccinium ovatum* (Evergreen huckleberry) **15.** *Osmanthus delavayi* **16.** *Viburnum davidii* **17.** *Euonymus fortunei* 'Vegeta' (Big-leaf winter creeper) **18.** Vegetables.

Design approach: The shape of this lot suits the owners' needs for a private entry and minimum front yard with an expanse in the rear for outdoor entertaining, relaxing, and children's play. Mass plantings, an entry court, and a wide driveway create an attractive entry requiring very little care. A generous wooden deck dominates the side yard. The lawn, sandbox, and most of the planting beds have an exposed aggregate border. Natives were emphasized in plant selection. A small area in the sun is set aside for growing vegetables. (Designed by A. Rex Zumwalt)

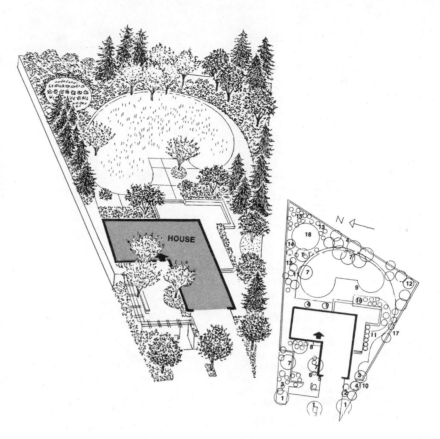

Dallas, Texas

LOW MAINTENANCE PLANTS: 1. *Yucca recurvifolia* (Yucca pendula) **2.** *Raphiolepis indica* (India hawthorn) **3.** *Trachelospermum asiaticum* (Asiatic Star jasmine) **4.** *Quercus virginiana* (Southern live oak) **5.** Lawn **6.** *Pinus thunbergiana* (Japanese black pine) **7.** *Magnolia grandiflora* (Southern magnolia) **8.** *Ilex cornuta* 'Burfordii' (Burford holly) **9.** *Photinia fraseri* **10.** *Liriope muscari* 'Majestic' (Lily turf) **11.** *Aucuba japonica* (Japanese aucuba) **12.** *Taxus cuspidata* (Japanese yew) **13.** *Hedera helix* (English ivy) **14.** *Fatsia japonica* (Aralia sieboldii, Japanese aralia) **15.** *Cleyera japonica* **16.** *Viburnum macrocephalum* 'Sterile' (Chinese snowball) **17.** *Pittosporum tobira* 'Variegata' (Tobira) **18.** *Ilex vomitoria* (Yaupon) **19.** *Cotoneaster glaucophylla* (Bright bead cotoneaster) **20.** *Quercus rubra* (Red oak) **21.** *Livistona chinensis* (Chinese fountain palm, Chinese fan palm) **22.** *Ilex cornuta* 'Rotunda' (Dwarf Chinese holly) **23.** *Lagerstroemia indica* (Crape myrtle) **24.** *Salix babylonica* (Weeping willow).

Design approach: Planting emphasizes low care plants with a Southwestern theme: yucca and cotoneaster, with boulders and pebbles for accents. Existing oak trees are incorporated in the design which includes a pool, cabana, and small courtyards for individual rooms. (Designed by Naud Burnett Associates)

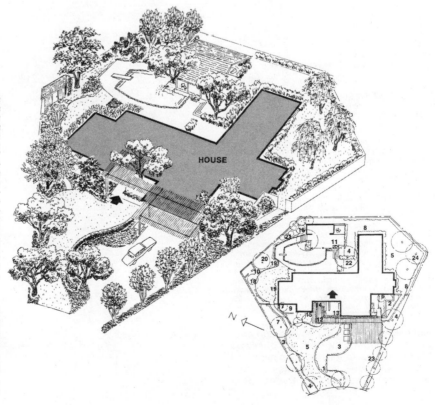

Westport, Connecticut

LOW MAINTENANCE PLANTS: 1. *Pachysandra terminalis* (Japanese spurge) **2.** *Taxus baccata* 'Repandens' (Spreading English yew) **3.** *Cornus florida* (Flowering dogwood) **4.** *Gleditsia triacanthos inermis* (Honey locust) **5.** *Cornus mas* (Cornelian cherry) **6.** *Ilex crenata* 'Helleri' (Japanese holly) **7.** *Hedera helix* (English ivy) **8.** Wisteria on arbor **9.** Clematis **10.** *Sophora japonica* (Japanese pagoda tree) **11.** *Vinca minor* (Dwarf periwinkle) **12.** *Betula verrucosa* (European white birch) **13.** *Pieris floribunda* (Mountain pieris) **14.** Evergreen azaleas **15.** *Vaccinium angustifolium* (Lowbush blueberry) **16.** *Oxydendrum arboreum* (Sorrel tree, Sourwood) **17.** *Tsuga caroliniana* (Carolina hemlock) **18.** *Viburnum plicatum tomentosum* (Doublefile viburnum) **19.** Deciduous azaleas **20.** *Potentilla* 'Katherine Dykes' **21.** *Taxus media* 'Hicksii' **22.** *Ajuga reptans* (Carpet bugle) **23.** Rhododendrons **24.** *Quercus palustris* (Pin oak).

Design approach: The enclosed drive and entry depend on shade-loving ground covers for a lush look under the pin oaks and flowering dogwoods. In the center of the pachysandra, a gravel area keeps weeds down and covers an area that would be hard to reach for watering. The rear garden is planned for views from the patios and the house. The curving lawn is surrounded by woodsy plants that provide a continuous color show without much care. (Designed by Jo Ray)

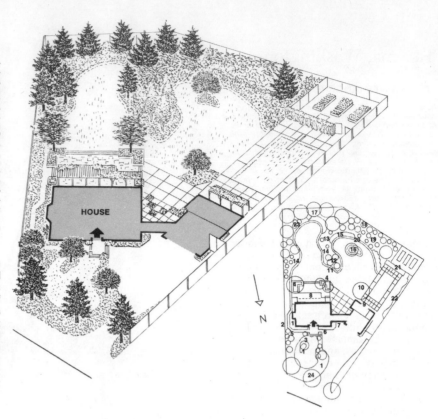

Denver, Colorado

LOW MAINTENANCE PLANTS: 1. *Pinus flexilis* (Limber pine) **2.** *Prunus besseyi* (Western sandcherry) **3.** *Elaeagnus angustifolia* (Russian olive) **4.** *Artemisia abrotanum* (Southernwood) **5.** *Gleditisia triacanthos* 'Skyline' (Honey locust) **6.** *Mahonia repens* (Creeping mahonia) **7.** *Juniperus chinensis* 'Hughes' (Hughes juniper) **8.** *Gymnocladus dioicus* (Kentucky coffee tree) **9.** *Hemerocallis* (Daylily) **10.** *Viburnum burkwoodii* (Burkwood viburnum) **11.** *Juniperus communis* (Pasture or oldfield juniper) **12.** *Sedum hybridum* (Stonecrop) **13.** *Fontanesia fortunei* **14.** *Euonymus fortunei* 'Colorata' (Purple-leaf winter creeper) **15.** *Potentilla verna* (Spring cinquefoil) **16.** *Pinus mugo mughus* (Mugho pine) **17.** *Populus tremuloides* (Quaking aspen) **18.** *Clematis jackmanii* (Jackman clematis) **19.** *Vinca minor* (Dwarf periwinkle) **20.** *Viburnum carlesii* (Korean spice viburnum) **21.** *Juniperus sabina* 'Tamariscifolia' (Tamarix juniper) **22.** *Quercus macrocarpa* (Bur oak) **23.** *Acer ginnala* (Ginnala maple) **24.** *Lysimachia nummularia* (Moneywort) **25.** *Rhus trilobata* (Sumac) **26.** *Ribes cereum* (Squaw currant) **27.** *Fallugia paradoxa* (Apache plume) **28.** *Populus sargentii* (Western cottonwood).

Design approach: A dry stream and flagstone paving combine with the plantings to evoke a mountain setting. An enclosed area is set aside for vegetables or children's play. (Designed by E. Alan Rollinger)

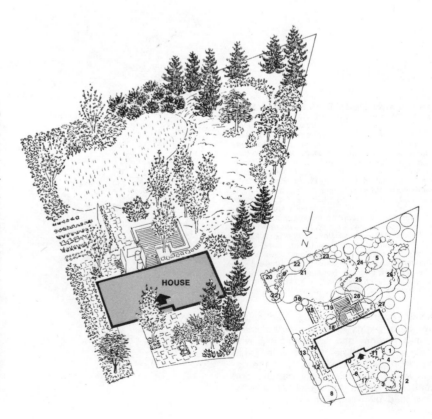

HILLSIDE LOT

Though a hillside lot is loaded with challenge, when it is carefully developed, it offers considerable variety of interest and a physical point of view that is endlessly fascinating.

A flat lot has its own drainage problems to be met (and they can be major). But on a hillside lot, water moves at a faster rate, so you must consider the hazard of erosion, along with the problem of leading water away from any buildings and into proper drainage passages on public rights of way. These matters are best planned for ahead of time. Attempting to dam an unwanted watercourse with a shovel and sand bags in the middle of a storm is most peoples' idea of a nightmare.

If the slope of your land is considerable, you'll be faced with the possible need for retaining walls, flights of steps, ramps, and subterranean or surface drainways. Finding the proper practical and aesthetic solutions to these problems will eliminate many maintenance issues. At the same time, you'll have added considerable interest to your garden.

Napa, California

LOW MAINTENANCE PLANTS: 1. *Ceanothus* 'Emily Brown' **2.** *Baccharis pilularis* (Dwarf coyote brush) **3.** *Acacia baileyana* (Bailey acacia) **4.** *Pittosporum tenuifolium* **5.** *Pinus canariensis* (Canary Island pine) **6.** *Pinus pinea* (Italian stone pine) **7.** *Pachysandra terminalis* (Japanese spurge) **8.** *Ceanothus griseus* (Carmel ceanothus) **9.** *Liquidambar styraciflua* (American sweetgum) **10.** *Pyracantha fortuneana* **11.** *Nandina domestica* (Heavenly bamboo) **12.** *Eucalyptus polyanthemos* (Silver dollar gum).

Design approach: Bringing the driveway up somewhat parallel to the street minimizes the slope and allows ample room for parking and maneuvering cars. Garage and work areas occupy this level, while the bedroom wing opens onto a garden at its level. Dining and living rooms both have doors to a sunny deck. Acacia, ceanothus, and baccharis, all of which are drought resistant, give scale and interest to the front but almost take care of themselves once they are established. They also provide seasonal color, along with the pyracantha and nandina. At the rear of the property, a grove of liquidambar rises up the hill, making a handsome background, especially in the fall. An open, sunny spot for vegetables is just out of view. (Designed by Roy Rydell)

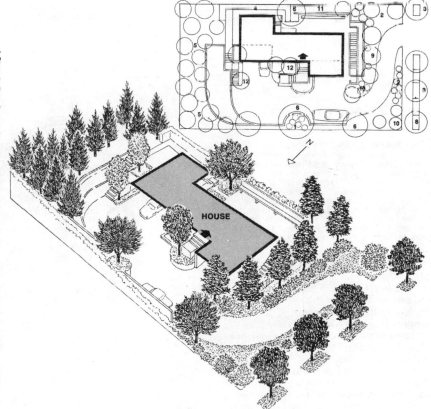

HOUSE

Portland, Oregon

LOW MAINTENANCE PLANTS: 1. *Cedrus deodara* (Deodar cedar) **2.** *Prunus serrulata* (Japanese flowering cherry) **3.** *Betula verrucosa* (European white birch) **4.** *Albizia julibrissin* (Silk tree) **5.** *Pinus contorta* (Shore pine, beach pine) **6.** *Cotoneaster dammeri* (Bearberry cotoneaster) **7.** Rhododendrons **8.** *Quercus palustris* (Pin oak) **9.** *Liquidambar styraciflua* (American sweetgum) **10.** *Vinca minor* (Dwarf periwinkle) **11.** Existing Douglas fir.

Design approach: As on most hillside lots, outdoor living space here is at a premium. A redwood deck solves this problem for this family with young children by providing facilities for entertaining, lounging, and play with a minimum of maintenance. Garden tools, patio furniture, and outdoor playthings can be stored under the deck. A blaze of spring color comes from the rhododendrons and flowering cherry. This is followed by the unusual pink flowers of the silk tree that last throughout the summer and are at their best viewed from above. Liquidambar bursts into fall color, and berries on the cotoneaster last into the winter. Cedars, pines, and Douglas fir give the garden a woodland feeling. Since most of the plants are viewed from the deck, they do not need the continual weeding and pruning required by those on more close-up view. (Designed by Chandler Fairbank)

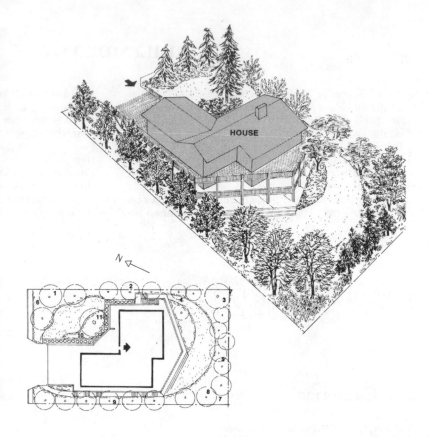

Seattle, Washington

LOW MAINTENANCE PLANTS: 1. *Cedrus deodara* (Deodar cedar) **2.** *Acer circinatum* (Vine maple) **3.** Rhododendron 'King George' **4.** *Mahonia aquifolium* 'Compacta' (Dwarf Oregon grape) **5.** *Viburnum davidii* **6.** *Enkianthus campanulatus* **7.** *Skimmia reevesiana* **8.** Rhododendron 'Anna Rose Whitney' **9.** *Ilex crenata* 'Convexa' **10.** *Cornus nuttallii* 'Goldspot' (Hybrid Pacific Dogwood) **11.** *Gaultheria shallon* 'Salal' **12.** *Viburnum plicatum tomentosum* (Doublefile viburnum) **13.** Annuals, bulbs **14.** Containers for seasonal color.

Design approach: Because this hillside lot provides a minimum of land on which to build the house, the hillside is pressed into service as a garden area. Mass planting is emphasized: groupings of rhododendrons; skimmia in beds; low-growing mahonia serving as ground cover. Brick-edged concrete, textured with labor-saving pea gravel finish, forms stairs, pathways, courtyard areas, and patio. Established natives already on hillside are complemented by planted natives: maples (in front), dogwood (blooming with showy color), and salal (adding transition from hillside to home). Deodar cedar gives woodsy effect. Outside dining area on garage roof is floored with wooden deck. (Designed by R. David Adams)

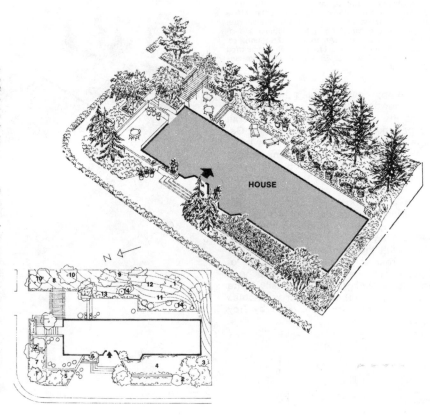

Sussex, Wisconsin

LOW MAINTENANCE PLANTS: 1. *Acer* (Maples) **2.** *Stephenandra incisa* 'Crispa' **3.** *Juniperus communis depressa* (Pasture or oldfield juniper) **4.** Naturalized narcissus and violets **5.** *Ajuga reptans* (Carpet bugle) **6.** Lawn **7.** Ash grove underplanted with ferns and violets **8.** *Euonymus fortunei* 'Colorata' (Purple-leaf winter creeper) **9.** *Taxus* (Yew) **10.** *Prunus americana* (American plum) **11.** Native shrubs, such as *Viburnum lentago* and *Cornus racemosa* (gray dogwood) **12.** *Impatiens walleriana* (Busy Lizzie) **13.** Herbs and vegetables in kitchen garden and service area **14.** *Malus* (Crabapple) **15.** Native sods (see below) **16.** Existing native woods: maple, oak, ash.

Design approach: A controlled return to nature is the key to low maintenance on a homesite carved out of a wooded Wisconsin hillside lot. A brick plateau around the home allows for traffic flow; a large drive and parking area make winter snow removal easier. The only concession to a lawn is over the septic system where tree roots would create a problem. Ground covers, such as ajuga and *Euonymus fortunei,* provide a year-round green carpet in other spots. Native sods that cover the hillside are pieces of the forest floor containing native wildflowers, grasses, and small shrubs cut out elsewhere and planted on the slope. The trees on the property were selected to blend with the surrounding native woods. (Designed by Thomas O. Lied)

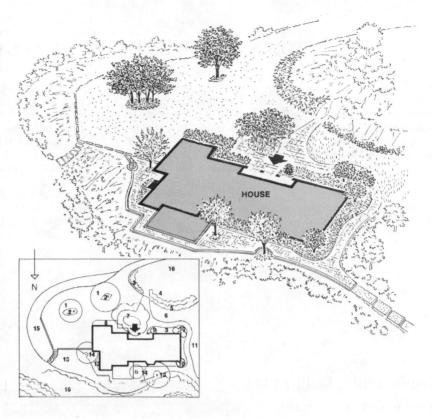

San Antonio, Texas

LOW MAINTENANCE PLANTS: 1. Native shrubs, trees, grasses, and ground covers. **2.** *Rosmarinus officinalis* 'Prostratus' (Dwarf Rosemary) **3.** *Trachelospermum asiaticum* (Asiatic star jasmine) **4.** *Pittosporum tobira* (Tobira) **5.** *Ficus pumila* (Creeping fig) **6.** *Raphiolepis indica* (India hawthorn) **7.** *Sophora secundiflora* (Mescal bean, Texas mountain laurel) **8.** *Ophiopogon japonicus* (Mondo grass) **9.** *Quercus virginiana* (Southern live oak) **10.** *Quercus texana* (Texas oak) **11.** *Hedera canariensis* (Algerian ivy).

Design approach: Large, sloping areas away from the house covered with native trees, shrubs, ground covers, and grasses are left as natural as possible, enhanced only by the addition of native ground covers to cut down on annual mowing of the grasses. Street and side areas are planted to provide privacy with natural-looking shrubs having minimum pruning requirements. Fast-growing ground covers quickly solve weed problems here. Smaller patio, deck, and entry areas closer to the house are more extensively planted. Container plants are often used here for seasonal splashes of color although the garden is complete without them. Native stone used in retaining walls adds to the natural appearance. (Designed by John O. Spice)

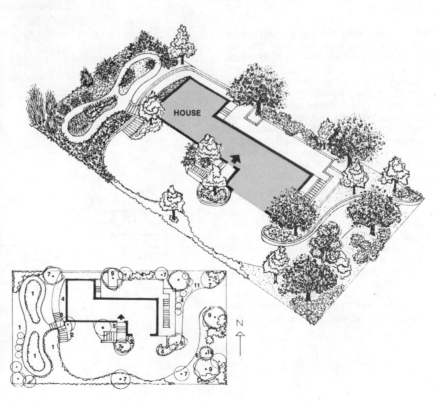

TOWN HOUSE LOT WITH SMALL GARDENS

More and more of us who have a yen for a low maintenance garden find that our actual garden size is ever more restricted. We may find that we have a postage stamp-sized balcony or that we are living in a townhouse with a pint-sized patio or atrium. This situation gives us the benefit of having less area to plant but the problem of not really knowing how to use small space to best advantage.

In such a minimum garden situation, we want to make space seem greater. We want our Lilliputian garden to take care of every outdoor wish we've ever dreamed of. Maintenance is not apt to be such a problem, for there isn't room to crowd in every plant and cutting we wish for. These are the gardens that we load with a collection of potted bulbs or annuals when we feel energetic and extravagant. (We cache them away when we feel more like lazing than watering or when we decide to go away on a long vacation.) Here is where we consider doubling the visual size of our garden with the use of mirror, false perspective treillage, or age-old secrets culled from an intensive study of Japanese garden illustrations.

Sacramento, California

LOW MAINTENANCE PLANTS: 1. *Malus floribunda* (Japanese flowering crabapple). **2.** *Lagerstroemia indica* (Crape myrtle) **3.** *Acer palmatum* (Japanese maple) **4.** *Trachelospermum jasminoides* (Star jasmine) **5.** *Sarcococca ruscifolia* **6.** *Fatsia japonica* (Japanese aralia) **7.** Southern indica azalea **8.** *Camellia sasanqua* **9.** *Actinidia chinensis* (Chinese gooseberry vine).

Design approach: Here is a town house set in a row of identical town houses, one jogged against the next to allow additional light and privacy for each. Opening onto a common area at right is a small, mainly paved entrance courtyard planted with three crape myrtles. In the rear (at left) is another court—so small it does little more than hold automobiles at bay. But this town house is blessed in its center with an atrium that brings additional light and air into the house. The atrium appears larger than it is because it is arranged on two levels (deck and patio) and has flooring of two contrasting textures (wood and concrete). Southern indica azaleas take a moderate amount of sun, survive California's warm, interior valley summers. A hardy ground cover, sarcococca has fragrant blossoms that enhance the small atrium area. Two plants — fatsia and actinidia — are used here because their bold scale contrasts effectively with other plants. (Designed by Roy Rydell)

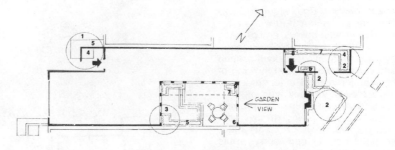

Tacoma, Washington

LOW MAINTENANCE PLANTS: 1. *Acer palmatum* (Japanese maple) **2.** *Mahonia nervosa* (Cascades mahonia) **3.** Southern Indica azalea 'Hino-crimson' **4.** Rhododendron 'Loder's White' **5.** *Fatsia japonica* (Japanese aralia) **6.** *Hydrangea anomala petiolaris* (Climbing hydrangea) **7.** Containers with annuals for seasonal color. **8.** Rhododendron 'Carita' **9.** *Cornus florida* (Flowering dogwood) **10.** Crocus.

Design approach: Brick paving covers most of the outdoors, including some of the living and entry areas, tying together the indoors and the outdoors. This, along with a glass wall at the rear of the living area, makes the court part of this room and gives a feeling of spaciousness. Plantings were arranged to create a changing vista from the living area, maintaining their continual good looks regardless of how little attention the garden receives. The flowering dogwood here is the focal point with year-round interest, from the profuse bloom in spring to its spectacular fall color and unusual winter twig pattern. Japanese maples, rhododendrons, and azaleas require little care in this area and make spectacular displays at different times of the year, as well as providing a year-round foliage backdrop. Raised beds for other plantings make care easier and set off the plants. (Designed by A. Rex Zumwalt)

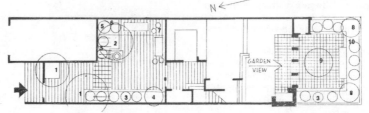

San Diego, California

LOW MAINTENANCE PLANTS: 1. *Hebe* 'Coed' **2.** *Clivia miniata* (Kaffir lily) **3.** *Begonia* 'Richmondensis' **4.** *Beloperone guttata* (Shrimp plant) (Plants 1-4 in containers) **5.** *Cissus rhombifolia* (Grape ivy) in hanging pot **6.** *Nandina domestica* (Heavenly bamboo) **7.** *Potentilla verna* (Spring cinquefoil) **8.** *Melaleuca quinquenervia* (Cajeput tree) **9.** *Pandorea jasminoides* (Bower vine) **10.** *Hemerocallis aurantiaca* (Golden summer daylily) **11.** *Hedera helix* 'Hahnii' (English ivy) **12.** *Eucalyptus sideroxylon* (Red ironbark, pink ironbark **13.** *Xylosma congestum.*

Design approach: In this garden area, a wooden deck provides an outdoor living space with few planting spots. This area receives intensive year-round use in this mild climate and must continually look attractive. Evergreen, low maintenance plants were selected as background materials. Many of these plants add their own seasonal interest, such as the eucalyptus with its bright pink flower clusters in the winter. Other seasonal color comes from container plants that are rotated throughout the year. The melaleuca tree provides an interesting, lacy form, casting light shade on the deck and offering yellow flowers throughout the summer and fall. (Designed by Todd Fry)

Milwaukee, Wisconsin

LOW MAINTENANCE PLANTS: 1. *Taxus media* 'Halloran' (Yew hedge) **2.** *Juniperus horizontalis* 'Wiltonii' (Blue carpet juniper) **3.** *Fraxinus pennsylvanica* 'Marshall' (Marshall seedless green ash) **4.** *Myrica pennsylvanica* (Bayberry) **5.** *Crataegus phaenopyrum* (Washington thorn) **6.** *Euonymus fortunei* 'Vegeta' (Big-leaf wintercreeper) **7.** *Amelanchier laevis* (Shadbush) **8.** *Pachysandra terminalis* (Japanese spurge) **9.** *Robinia* (Locust) **10.** *Malus* 'Red Splendor' (Flowering crabapple) **11.** *Pinus aristata* (Bristlecone pine) **12.** *Acer ginnala* (Amur maple) **13.** *Cornus mas* (Cornelian cherry) **14.** *Fragaria chiloensis* (Wild strawberry).

Design approach: The small outdoor space here is designed for maximum use with minimum care. Disease-resistant plant varieties were selected for seasonal interest throughout the year, beginning with the early flowering Cornelian cherry. Junipers take the place of a lawn as the evergreen mainstay of the garden—especially important because there is limited storage space for the garden equipment a lawn requires. All construction materials have either a permanent finish or are used in a weathered form. Brick set in concrete with heating coils eliminates the snow removal chore and use of salt as a de-icer (salt is injurious to plants). (Designed by Patricia Davis)

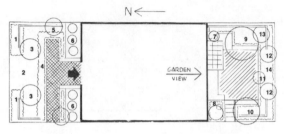

Freeport, New York

LOW MAINTENANCE PLANTS: 1. *Juniperus chinensis* 'Pfitzeriana' (Pfitzer juniper) **2.** *Elaeagnus angustifolia* (Russian olive) **3.** *Pyracantha coccinea* (Firethorn) **4.** *Cedrus atlantica* (Atlas cedar) **5.** *Juniperus horizontalis* 'Wiltonii' (Blue carpet juniper) **6.** *Juniperus procumbens* 'Nana' (Japanese garden juniper) **7.** *Taxus media* 'Hicksii' **8.** *Juniperus chinensis* 'Torulosa' (Hollywood juniper) **9.** *Juniperus sabina* 'Tamariscifolia' (Tamarix juniper) **10.** *Taxus baccata* (English yew) **11.** *Gleditsia triacanthos inermis* (Honey locust) **12.** *Ilex glabra* (Bayberry, inkberry) **13.** *Ilex pendunculosa* (Cherry holly) **14.** Espaliered *cotoneaster horizontalis* (Rock cotoneaster) **15.** *Pinus thunbergiana* (Japanese black pine) **16.** *Amelanchier laevis* (Shadbush) **17.** *Pachysandra terminalis* (Japanese spurge) **18.** *Pinus mugo mughus* (Mugho pine) **19.** *Cedrus atlantica* 'Glauca' (Blue atlas cedar) **20.** Espaliered *pyracantha coccinea* (Firethorn) **21.** Merion Kentucky and Kentucky bluegrass sod lawn.

Design approach: Ornamental pilings, brick paving, and railroad tie edging set the theme for this garden. Washed, 2-inch beach gravel on polyethylene film in planting beds prevents weed growth and controls moisture in the soil. A 6-foot-high transparent glass screen provides shelter for plants and a year-round outdoor living area. (Designed by Rudi Harbauer)

Designs for Specific Garden Areas

Low maintenance landscape designs on the previous 21 pages have concentrated on entire lots of various shapes. But on the following 15 pages, designers have focused down to the specific garden areas that surround most homes. These include the front garden, parking area garden, entry garden, kitchen garden, and rear garden.

In this section, too, the approach is different. Each example consists of two sketches—on the left, one showing plantings and a design that require generally high maintenance; on the right, one showing the garden re-designed and replanted for low maintenance care.

Because these sketches picture your yard in small sections, you may be encouraged to begin a *gradual* redesigning and replanting of your property rather than being discouraged by the need to begin a *total* renovation. And, of course, by studying *all* the sketches rather than just the ones for your area, you can readily adapt design ideas from any part of the country, substituting plant materials for your region from the charts on pages 64-93.

FRONT GARDEN

Most homes have two distinctly different areas—public and private—more commonly referred to as front and back yard. In apportioning his garden work, a home owner often feels an especially strong responsibility to make his front garden something of which he (and his neighbors) can be proud. A front garden can present an attractive face to the world, though, without requiring hours of effort to mow, prune, weed, and water.

On the following three pages, landscape designers have created low maintenance plans for you to study. Each designer has provided a "before" and "after" sketch, showing how a relatively high maintenance (but not necessarily poorly designed) front garden can be transformed into a low maintenance one.

Santa Cruz, California

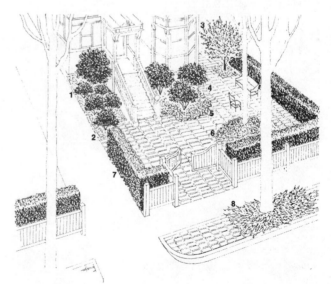

BEFORE: 1. *Syringa* (Lilac) 2. Forsythia 3. Mixed annuals 4. Iris 5. Rock plants 6. Roses 7. *Buxus microphylla* (Boxwood).

Problems: Irregular-shaped lawn requires hand clipping; lawn is scarred by traffic patterns. Rose bed requires watering, spraying, pruning, fertilizing. Hedge needs regular pruning. Mixed annuals planting calls for varied watering, pruning, and feeding schedule. Perennials require cutting back, regular division, feeding. Rock plants need separate attention. The garden lacks an evergreen backbone.

AFTER (lower maintenance): 1. Azalea 2. *Pachysandra terminalis* (Japanese spurge) 3. *Malus scheideckeri* (Scheidecker crabapple) 4. Southern Indica azalea 5. *Fragaria chiloensis* (Wild strawberry) 6. *Cistus salvifolius* (Sageleaf rockrose) 7. *Rhamnus alaternus* (Italian buckthorn. 8. *Juniperus horizontalis* "Wiltonii" (Blue Carpet juniper).

Solutions: Brick-on-sand paving eliminates lawn care and traffic patterns worn into grass. Fence and slow-growing hedge keep out blowing rubbish and dust. Mixed annuals and perennials are replaced with simple evergreen ground covers. (Design: Roy Rydell)

Portland, Oregon

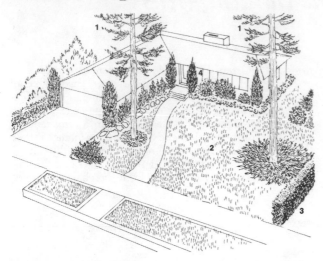

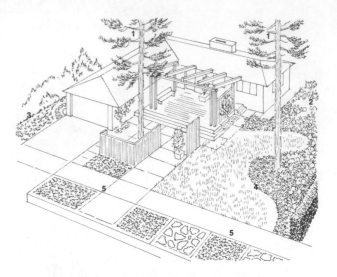

BEFORE: 1. *Abies concolor* (White fir) 2. Lawn 3. *Prunus laurocerasus* (English laurel) 4. *Cedrus libani* (Cedar of Lebanon).

Problems: A large lawn area and clipped shrubs create maintenance problems for the owners. They wanted a more informal look and a more sheltered and welcoming entry. They also asked for seasonal color without having to plant annuals.

AFTER (lower maintenance): 1. *Abies concolor* (White fir) 2. Rhododendrons 3. *Viburnum davidii* 4. Azaleas 5. *Vinca minor*.

Solutions: Structural elements take the place of the more time-consuming plantings and create a new entry sheltered from the winter rain and hot summer sun. The flowering shrubs and even the vinca ground cover provide successive bloom without the work of annuals. These shrubs need only occasional pruning, summer watering, and annual feeding. (Design: Chandler D. Fairbank)

Dallas, Texas

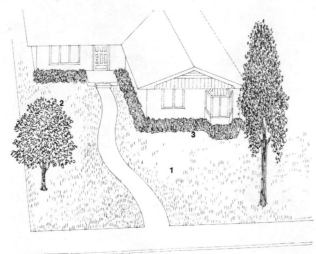

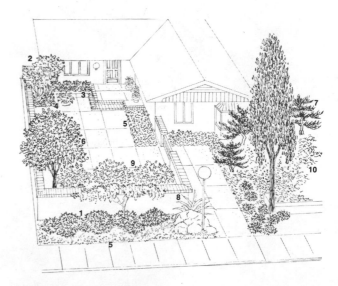

BEFORE: 1. Lawn 2. *Quercus rubra* (Red oak) 3. *Ligustrum japonicum* (Waxleaf privet).

Problems: The lack of privacy and the incessant demands of an extensive lawn area are two drawbacks to this yard. Homeowners wanted to shield their bedroom from the street, get rid of the fast-growing waxleaf privet hedge. This front garden has the additional handicap of no seasonal color.

AFTER (lower maintenance): 1. *Ilex vomitoria* (Dwarf yaupon) 2. *Lagerstroemia indica* (Crape myrtle) 3. *Raphiolepis indica* (India hawthorn) 4. *Liriope muscari* (Big blue lily turf) 5. *Trachelospermum asiaticum* (Asiatic jasmine) 6. *Quercus rubra* (Red oak) 7. *Pinus thunbergiana* (Japanese black pine) 8. *Yucca recurvifolia* 9. *Pittosporum tobira* (Tobira) 10. *Gelsemium sempervirens* (Carolina jessamine).

Solutions: A brick wall screens the yard from the street; the pine screens the bedroom window. Jasmine ground cover replaces grass. (Design: Naud Burnett Associates)

Denver, Colorado

BEFORE: 1. *Sorbus aucuparia* (European mountain ash) 2. Lawn 3. Spruce 4. Existing shrubs.

Problems: Spruce trees create a great deal of litter on the lawn and paved areas. The size of the lawn makes it very time-consuming to maintain. Shrubs were planted without a plan, many of them too close together, and now it is a pruning chore to keep them away from walks, windows, and each other. Many of the shrubs are not adapted to Denver's climate.

AFTER (lower maintenance): 1. *Sorbus aucuparia* (European mountain ash) 2. *Gleditsia triacanthos inermis* 'Skyline' (Honey locust) 3. *Pinus mugo mughus* (Mugho pine) 4. *Juniperus horizontalis* (Prostrata juniper) 5. *Mahonia repens* (Creeping mahonia) 6. *Pinus aristata* (Bristle-cone pine).

Solutions: The lawn size was reduced, creating more paved areas for easier traffic circulation. Shrubs and trees in scale with the house and suited to the location reduce pruning and look good year round. (Design: E. Alan Rollinger)

Westport, Connecticut

BEFORE: 1. Multiflora rose 2. *Philadelphus* (Mock orange) 3. *Spiraea* 4. Syringa (Lilac) 5. *Chaenomeles japonica* (Japanese quince) 6. *Berberis thunbergii* (Japanese barberry) 7. Roses 8. Rhododendron 9. *Taxus cuspidata* (Japanese yew) 10. *Ligustrum ibolium* (Privet) 11. *Forsythia suspensa* 12. Lawn 13. *Acer* (Maple) 14. *Paeonia* (Peony).

Problems: Mock orange and multiflora rose offer no privacy; other shrubs are scattered without design or unity. The view from a window is blocked by the privet. The lawn is in poor condition, and shrubs and stepping stones are difficult to mow around.

AFTER (lower maintenance): 1. *Viburnum* 2. *Euonymus alata* 3. Espaliered *Pyracantha coccinea* (Firethorn) 4. *Malus baccata* (Siberian crabapple) 5. *Pachysandra terminalis* 6. *Euonymus fortunei* 'Kewensis' 7. *Ilex vomitoria* 'Stokes' 8. *Vinca minor* 9. *Buxus microphylla koreana* (Korean boxwood) 10. *Clematis* 11. *Juniperus sabina* 'Tamariscifolia' (Tamarix juniper).

Solutions: A broad, brick terrace eliminates lawn, creates a pleasant patio area. Fence and shrubs provide privacy from the road. Clematis offers shade in summer and lets light through in winter. (Design: Jo Ray)

PARKING AREA GARDEN

Let's face it, our mobile world today centers around the automobile, and we must provide for its maneuvering and storage. Though parking areas are mainly utilitarian, sometimes they can serve a double function, providing a play area for children or badminton court for adults.

Learn to appreciate what help the shade and shadow pattern of overhead trees will be in enriching the bleakness of the blacktop or concrete needed for the parked vehicle. If possible, provide a screen of growth, a berm, or fencing to keep the glitter of chrome and enamel from dominating the domestic setting. Give a car the space it needs and adequate adjacent pavement, so that getting in and out with the groceries will not be difficult for people nor destructive to the lawn or shrubs nearby. Arrange for parking to be located where it is convenient for the delivery of both packages and passengers—but try to give these areas the illusion of a low maintenance park rather than of a parking lot.

San Diego, California

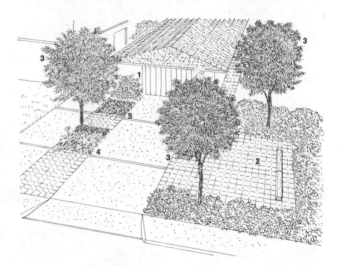

BEFORE: 1. *Xylosma congestum* **2.** *Raphiolepis indica* **3.** Concrete pads with grass strips **4.** *Jacaranda acutifolia* **5.** *Potentilla verna* (Spring cinquefoil) **6.** *Nandina domestica* (Heavenly bamboo).

Problems: Spaces around concrete pads in the extra parking area and driveway are planted with turf to cut down on glare and maintain a green appearance. All of this turf requires mowing and edging. Leaves and blossoms from the jacaranda tree must be raked up. Shrubs need occasional pruning.

AFTER (lower maintenance): 1. *Pittosporum tobira* (Tobira) **2.** Stamped concrete with railroad tie wheel stop **3.** *Podocarpus gracillor* (Fern pine) **4.** *Clivia miniata* (Kaffir lily) **5.** *Potentilla verna* (Spring cinquefoil).

Solutions: Parking area in stamped concrete cuts glare and may be washed down easily. Railroad tie is bolted into concrete as a wheel stop. The podocarpus are clean, pest free, and need only occasional shaping. Pittosporum and the potentilla ground cover require little maintenance. (Design: Todd Fry)

Seattle, Washington

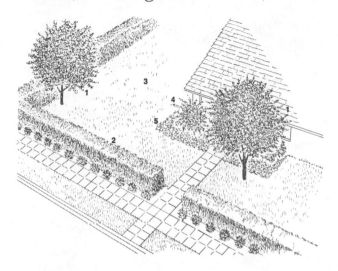

BEFORE: 1. *Ulmus parvifolia* (Chinese elm) 2. *Prunus laurocerasus* (English laurel) 3. Lawn 4. *Deutzia* 5. *Spiraea.*

Problems: Most of the plants are deciduous, giving no winter interest to the garden; they all have grown fast and are out of scale with the house. The Chinese elm is not a good lawn tree because its shallow roots monopolize moisture and nutrients. The large lawn, which extends to the parking strip, takes a great deal of care. Parking is on the street only.

AFTER: 1. *Skimmia reevesiana* 2. Dwarf rhododendrons 3. *Hedera helix* 'Hahn's self branching' (Hahn's ivy) 4. *Acer palmatum* (Japanese maple) 5. *Raphiolepis umbellata* 6. *Nandina domestica* (Heavenly bamboo) 7. *Prunus serrulata* 'Amanogawa' (Flowering cherry) 8. *Ternstroemia gymnanthera* 9. *Prunus cerasifera* 'Krauter Vesuvius' 10. Rhododendrons.

Solutions: Brick-on-sand paving and fence create a private entry with easy access from a new parking area. Small trees and low shrubs fit the scale of the house and reduce pruning. (Design: Glen Hunt)

Houston, Texas

BEFORE: 1. *Buxus microphylla japonica* (Japanese boxwood) 2. *Liriope* (Lily turf) 3. *Taxus cuspidata* (Japanese yew) 4. *Ligustrum japonicum* (Japanese privet) 5. Lawn.

Problems: Because they do lots of entertaining along a busy street, homeowners here needed to provide additional parking. They also wanted to enhance their front yard and to provide space for children's play. Clipped boxwood hedges and poodle trees make for demanding garden care.

AFTER (lower maintenance): 1. *Raphiolepis indica* (India hawthorn) 2. *Nandina domestica* 'Nana' (Dwarf heavenly bamboo) 3. *Moraea iridioides* (Evergreen iris) 4. *Taxus cuspidata* (Japanese yew) 5. St. Augustine grass 6. *Lagerstroemia indica* (Crape myrtle) 7. *Ajuga reptans* (Carpet bugle) 8. *Quercus nigra* (Water oak) 9. *Quercus virginiana* (Southern live oak) 10. *Liriope muscari* (Big blue lily turf).

Solutions: Designers provided an easy-care, off-street parking court. Added paving decreases upkeep. Raphiolepis is slow growing; nandina takes severe pruning well. Trees give shade to house, cars. (Design: A. Gregory Catlow)

Orlando, Florida

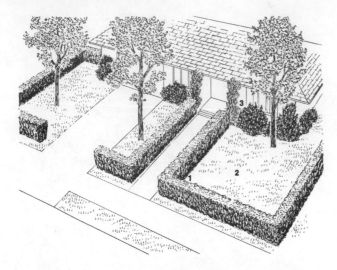

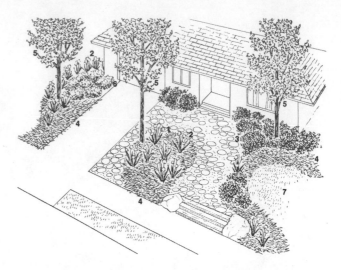

BEFORE: 1. Shaped hedge 2. St. Augustine grass 3. Overgrown shrubs.

Problems: Shaped hedges around the lawn need constant trimming to look neat, vary in maintenance requirements. These hedges surround a lawn and shrink the front yard, not allowing for full use of this area. Shrubs planted under the windows have grown up and are starting to block the windows. Plantings interfere with yard's original circulation pattern.

AFTER (lower maintenance): 1. *Liriope muscari* (Big blue lily turf) 2. *Moraea iridiodes* 3. *Xylosma congestum* 4. *Juniperus squamata* 'Parsonii' 5. *Liquidambar styraciflua* 6. Azaleas 7. Bahia sod.

Solutions: This area was opened up for easier access and viewing. Cypress rounds with cypress mulch make an interesting, low maintenance entry walk. Plants such as liriope and junipers add year-round interest with little care. St. Augustine grass is replaced with Bahia sod—a better performer near the coast in Eastern Florida. (Design: Herbert Ramsaier, Scott Girard)

Atlanta, Georgia

BEFORE: 1. Steep hill covered with lawn 2. Gravel walk 3. Exposed garbage cans 4. Parking

Problems: The driveway of this home comes around to the rear yard, meeting a treeless, grass-covered hill up to the house. The owners wanted to use this sunny side of their home for outdoor living as well as for growing herbs, vegetables, and fruit trees. Two other needs: storage space hidden from the outdoor living area, and easier access to the house than the gravel path provides.

AFTER (lower maintenance): 1. Deck 2. Peach tree 3. Vegetables in raised beds 4. Apple tree 5. Mint in planter 6. Walk of native stone 7. Storage, garbage 8. Herbs.

Solutions: A deck creates an outdoor living area with room under it for storage. A peach tree screens the view of the parking area. Vegetables and herbs are in raised beds for easier care. Native stone was used as a retaining wall under the deck and as a maintenance-free walk; the driveway and planters are edged with the same stone. (Design: Barbara Cunningham)

ENTRY GARDEN

No matter how low in maintenance you plan to make your entry garden (and this is often the place where the minimum will do), it should not be cramped. It should say "Welcome." An entrance can be like an outdoor room, leading the visitor effortlessly and pleasantly from the front yard into the interior of the residence. It is enjoyable to have a semi-private place to say "Hello" and "Goodbye" out of the range of passing traffic.

The entrance should be in keeping with the architectural design of the house. Don't transform a saltbox or a Monterey adobe with a flying portico straight out of a World's Fair, and don't attempt to turn a building of considerable scale into an English cottage. Respect the integrity of what exists. If what exists is overblown or in poor taste, though, remove the damage and simplify or, if necessary, conceal it.

Santa Barbara, California

BEFORE: 1. Tree roses 2. Annuals 3. Lawn 4. Perennial border (delphinium, foxglove, coreopsis, iris) 5. Container plants (fuchsia, begonia, ferns) 6. *Buxus microphylla koreana* (Korean boxwood) 7. *Eugenia paniculata* 8. *Ligustrum japonicum* 'Texanum' (Japanese privet) 9. Geraniums in containers.

Problems: Lawn care is made difficult by the shade from the two story house, lack of a mowing strip, and a traffic pattern between the wall and veranda. Container plants, annual beds, and tree roses need continual attention. Gravel on the path must be continually swept back into place.

AFTER (lower maintenance): 1. *Agave attenuata* 2. Flagstones dry-laid in decomposed granite 3. Flagstone in concrete 4. Decomposed granite 5. *Aloe arborescens* (Tree aloe) 6. *Rhapis humilis* (Lady palm) 7. *Phaedranthus buccinatorius* (Blood-red trumpet vine) 8. *Strelitzia nicolai* (Giant bird of paradise) 9. *Gelsemium sempervirens* (Carolina jessamine) 10. *Arctostaphylos densiflora* 'Howard McMinn' (Manzanita).

Solutions: Flagstone in brown-colored concrete creates a single livable area out of the veranda and entry. In areas with decomposed granite, a pre-emergent herbicide was applied the first year to eliminate weeds. All plants need only occasional watering and pruning and are grouped for easier care. (Design: Isabelle Greene Haller)

Phoenix, Arizona

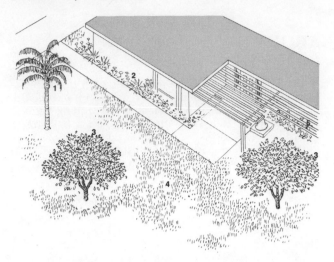

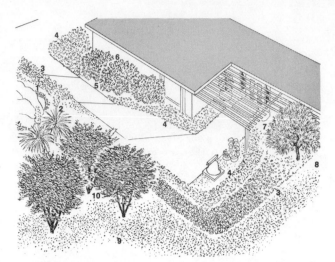

BEFORE: **1.** *Arecastrum romanzoffianum* (Queen palm) **2.** Annuals **3.** *Morus alba* (White mulberry) **4.** Bermuda grass **5.** *Podocarpus gracilior* (Fern pine).

Problems: Podocarpus is too large to be under overhang. The owners wanted plants more appropriate to a desert setting. Mulberry trees are difficult to clean up after on a lawn. The palm is vulnerable to breaking in high winds in this unprotected exposure. Bermuda grass does not stay green all winter. Runoff from the overhang drips into flower beds causing plants to be overwatered.

AFTER (lower maintenance): **1.** *Sempervivum tectorum* (Hens and chickens) **2.** *Yucca recurvifolia* **3.** *Lantana montevidensis* **4.** *Potentilla verna* (Spring cinquefoil) **5.** Bark mulch **6.** *Leucophyllum frutescens* (Texas ranger) **7.** *Cercidium floridum* (Blue palo verde) **8.** *Larrea divaricata* (Creosote bush) **9.** Brown decomposed granite. **10.** *Prosopis glandulosa torreyana* (Mesquite).

Solutions: The lawn is eliminated, a desert theme is carried out, access from driveway is easier. Infrequent watering is the only maintenance once plants are established. (Design: F. J. MacDonald & Associates)

Dallas, Texas

BEFORE: **1.** Brick stepping stones **2.** Seasonal flowers **3.** *Sedum* **4.** Espaliered *Camellia sasanqua* **5.** *Ilex cornuta* 'Burfordii' (Burford holly) **6.** *Camellia sasanqua* **7.** *Quercus rubra* (Red oak).

Problems: Lawn around brick stepping stones needs hand trimming, continually invades the ground cover. Sedum requires trimming and doesn't take foot traffic well. Seasonal flowers call for continual attention and replacement. Espaliered camellia needs training.

AFTER (lower maintenance): **1.** Brick walk **2.** *Camellia sasanqua* 'White Dove' **3.** *Ilex vomitoria* 'Nana' (Dwarf yaupon) **4.** *Quercus rubra* (Red oak) **5.** *Quercus virginiana* (Southern live oak) **6.** *Raphiolepis indica* (India hawthorn).

Solutions: Brick headers between exposed aggregate pads replaced sedum to eliminate trimming, allow foot traffic. Brick walk instead of stepping stones makes mowing, walking easier, stops grass from invading plant bed. Seasonal plantings replace permanent ones. Raphiolepis, dwarf yaupon, camellias stay low, need little pruning. (Design: Erika Farkac)

Seattle, Washington

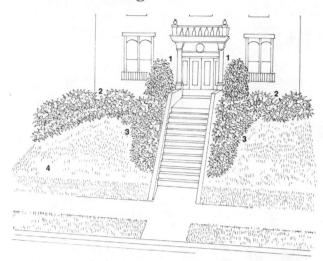

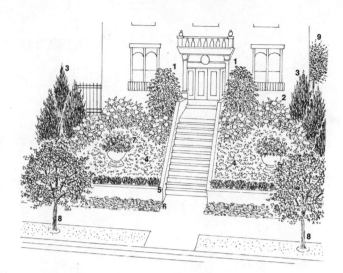

BEFORE: 1. *Magnolia grandiflora* 'Majestica' (Southern magnolia) **2.** Rhododendrons **3.** Azaleas **4.** Lawn.

Problems: The sloping lawn is difficult to mow and keep evenly green. It is too open to the street to be used for sitting or play. Litter from the magnolias will need to be raked from the lawn. The entry has no privacy from the street; the sparse plantings make the house seem even closer to the street than it is.

AFTER (lower maintenance): 1. Existing magnolias **2.** Rhododendrons **3.** *Cupressus sempervirens* 'Stricta' (Columnar Italian cypress) **4.** Azaleas **5.** *Buxus sempervirens* 'Suffruticosa' (True dwarf boxwood) **6.** *Hedera helix* (English Ivy) **7.** *Chrysanthemum frutescens* (Marguerite) in urns **8.** *Platanus acerifolia* (London plane tree) **9.** *Ulmus parvifolia* (Chinese elm).

Solutions: Lawn was replaced with low, compact azaleas. Slow growing, formal-looking shrubs enclose the garden. (Design: R. David Adams)

Sussex, Wisconsin

BEFORE: 1. Flagstone steps in poor lawn **2.** Overgrown shrubs **3.** *Ulmus* (Elm) **4.** Clump of large birch trees **5.** Bushy, spreading evergreens **6.** Upright arborvitae **7.** Annuals.

Problems: Parts of the front and side lawn are in too much shade to do well; the lawn next to the drive was ruined by snow plowing and salting. Hand trimming is required next to the fence. Roses and annuals need continual care.

AFTER (lower maintenance): 1. Lawn **2.** Brick walk **3.** Existing elm tree with pebble mulch, raised brick **4.** Brick mowing strip **5.** Existing birch clump **6.** *Taxus cuspidata* (Spreading yews) **7.** *Euonymus fortunei* 'Colorata' **8.** *Pachysandra terminalis* (Japanese spurge) **9.** *Euonymus fortunei* 'Vegeta' **10.** *Taxus media* 'Brownii' (Globe yew) **11.** *Amelanchier laevis* (Sarvis tree).

Solutions: Mowing and snow removal are easier with the new brick; lawn in heavy shade is eliminated. Brick curbs around planting beds prevent soil from washing onto the walk. (Design: Thomas O. Lied)

KITCHEN GARDEN

Perhaps outside your kitchen door you have enough space to take care of some of the auxiliary functions of this room and the utility rooms apt to be nearby. If you've decided that a vegetable garden is in order, it's nice to have it, along with a patch of herbs, within easy reach of the stove. If you like to shuck peas outside on a pleasant day, provide a comfortable place to sit. See that there is a convenient and orderly place to store tools nearby. You'll want to have refuse containers close at hand but screened from view. If airing clothing or bedding is part of your routine, set aside space that is handy and ready. Perhaps this area will do double duty when put to use for building projects and other hobbies. A kitchen garden is also a logical place for a potting bench—even for a lath house or small greenhouse.

Farther removed from the kitchen, screened from the more mundane utility area, consider setting aside a comfortable and attractive space for outdoor dining, a spot where one can linger after a meal, contemplating as the changing light transforms your garden picture.

Fresno, California

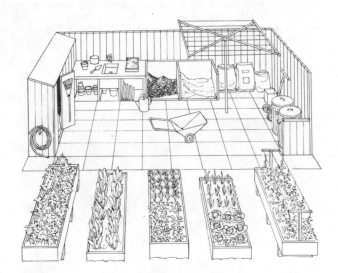

BEFORE: Vegetables: Lettuce, corn, peppers, cabbage.

Problems: A muddy and disorganized area outside the kitchen is surrounded by a hedge that is ragged and bare at the bottom because of lack of attention. There is no place to store tools and other garden work materials. Vegetable varieties planted here need special care, especially in the poorly drained soil.

AFTER (lower maintenance): Vegetables: tomatoes, swiss chard, beets, carrots, onions, lettuce, beans.

Solutions: An unpainted redwood fence requiring virtually no maintenance replaces the hedge. An attached storage shed gives a weatherproof home to tools and sprays. Added are a convenient work bench with a sink and bins for compost and soil amendments. Raised beds increase drainage and ease back bending. Paving eliminates weeds. (Design: Roy Rydell)

Long Grove, Illinois

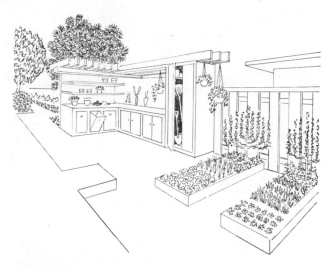

Before: Lawn in tight areas needs hand trimming. Foot traffic to front yard creates path through lawn. Flower and vegetable beds are inaccessible from one side. No work or storage space is provided for tools, soil amendments. Present yard exposes poor views and gives no privacy.

AFTER (lower maintenance): Asphalt replaces lawn for lower maintenance, easy clean up. Raised, separated planting beds for flowers and vegetables allow easy access from all sides. Tool storage, soil bins, work table with shelves provide orderly work area. Trellis with plexiglas panel deflects rain, creates partial shade, holds hanging pots. Fence screens poor views, increases privacy, gives surface to espalier vegetables (tomatoes) or fruits (dwarf apples). (Design: Theodore Brickman Company)

Seattle, Washington

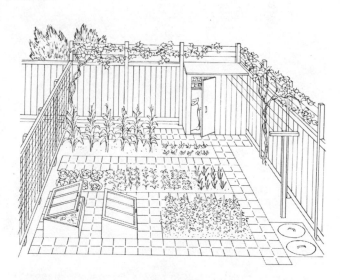

BEFORE: The space here is limited, but the spot is too sunny and too close to the house to be wasted. It is also constantly on view from the house, yet is so handy that it has become a catchall for tools and garbage, making the area an eyesore. Plants don't do well here because of poor soil and a slight slope that makes watering difficult. The owners like to start plants here from seed or cuttings, but pots and flats usually get lost in the disorganized shuffle.

AFTER (lower maintenance): A fence encloses the area, holds grape vines, and forms one side of a tool storage shed. The enclosure isolates the area from the rest of the garden, enabling the owners to neglect the vegetables between crops. Garbage disposal is convenient to the kitchen but is now hidden from view by sunken receptacles. Raised beds allow for soil amendments and correct the slope for easier watering. Cold frames give seedlings an early, sheltered start. (Design: Glen Hunt)

San Antonio, Texas

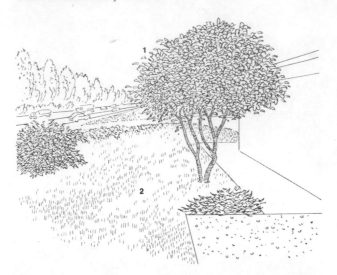

BEFORE: 1. *Diospyros texana* (Texas persimmon tree) **2.** Lawn.

Problems: The large expanse of lawn requires a great deal of care and is completely open to the street. A pleasant shade tree offers some relief from the afternoon sun in the kitchen window, but the lack of privacy discourages sitting under it. Nothing here invites people outdoors.

AFTER (lower maintenance): 1. *Lagerstroemia indica* (Crape myrtle) **2.** *Raphiolepis indica* (India hawthorn) **3.** *Ajuga reptans* (Carpet bugle) **4.** *Diospyros texana* (Texas persimmon tree).

Solutions: Brick wall and crape myrtle trees block view of street and create a private outdoor living area. Mexican tile paving makes a practical surface for outdoor dining in the shade of the persimmon tree. The tree also provides filtered shade for the plants below it. (Design: Glenn Cook)

Scottsdale, Arizona

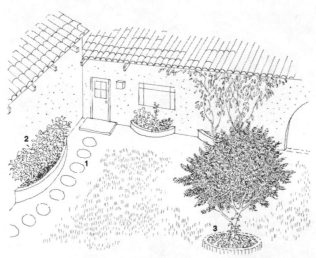

BEFORE: 1. Concrete stepping stones in lawn leading to fuse boxes. **2.** Roses **3.** Raised planter around tree.

Problems: Lawn is difficult to mow with concrete stepping stones and planters interspersed, and its use is restricted when broken up like this. Plants grown in the concrete planters are not appropriate for this area and struggle in the summer heat.

AFTER (lower maintenance): 1. Brick pavers **2.** Raised planter for herbs, vegetables **3.** Palm **4.** Lawn **5.** *Prosopis glandulosa torreyana* (Mesquite) **6.** *Cercidium floridum* (Blue palo verde) **7.** *Eriobotrya deflexa* (Bronze loquat) **8.** *Gardenia jasminoides* 'Veitchii' **9.** *Santolina chamae-cyparissus* (Lavender cotton).

Solutions: The lawn is used for bocce ball; a wooden seat around the planter accommodates spectators. Vegetables are given ideal conditions in raised beds and full sun. (Design: F. J. MacDonald and Associates)

REAR GARDEN

No part of your garden is an isolated entity. This is particularly true of your rear garden. Though you may wish to screen one part from another in a purposeful way, you should be able to move from one area to another with grace, convenience, and pleasure. As a rule, if the eye is stopped by a tree or a hedge as it searches for the limit of a garden's vista, the illusion of space is increased and the delight in discovering the concealed space is enhanced.

In planning your low maintenance rear garden, don't forget to consider what it looks like from within the house. You have an opportunity to create a special world capable of increasing your indoor pleasures throughout the year. In doing this, consider your neighbor; place barriers in areas that will insure his privacy as well as yours. But be considerate, too, of his desire for shade or need of sun when you plant trees that will grow to great size.

Berkeley, California

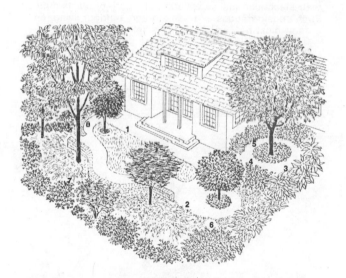

BEFORE: 1. Lawn 2. Perennial bed 3. Rhododendrons 4. Camellias 5. Southern indica Azaleas 6. *Rhamnus alaternus* (Italian buckthorn) 7. *Fremontodendron* (Flannel bush) 8. *Cistus hybridus* (White rockrose).

Problems: This garden grew without a plan, so plants with different requirements are grouped together. Size at maturity was not considered, so shrubs are crowded and compete for moisture and nutrients. The lawn always looks ragged since it requires frequent hand clipping around trees, shrubs, and stepping stones.

AFTER (lower maintenance): 1. Lawn 2. *Cotoneaster dammeri radicans* (Bearberry cotoneaster) 3. Rhododendrons 4. *Camellia japonica* 5. Southern indica azaleas 6. *Rhamnus alaternus* (Italian buckthorn) 7. *Fremontodendron* (Flannel bush) 8. *Cistus hybridus* (White rockrose).

Solutions: Shrubs are regrouped more compatibly, with the shade and moisture-loving camellias, azaleas, and rhododendrons together and the sun-loving, drought resistant plants off where they can take care of themselves. Paving separates the lawn from the trees and shrubs. (Design: Roy Rydell)

San Marino, California

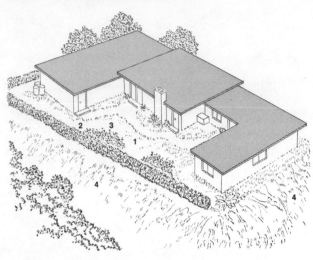

BEFORE: **1.** Lawn **2.** Hedge **3.** Annual bed **4.** Eroded slope.

Problems: Owners coping with a southern exposure need privacy and sun protection that still allow a view of the valley. Though erosion control is required on the slopes, their steepness makes watering and care of plants difficult. Such considerations as trash storage, outdoor living, and a garden must be combined in a small area.

AFTER (lower maintenance): **1.** *Hymenosporum flavum* (Sweetshade) **2.** *Hedera helix* 'Needle Point' **3.** *Xylosma congestum* **4.** *Ternstroemia gymnanthera* **5.** Azaleas **6.** Concrete paving with a salt finish.

Solutions: A stained wood fence at the rear of the level area encloses a service area and affords some privacy. Needlepoint ivy helps to retain the slope. An automatic watering system was installed to water this, along with the trees and shrubs. The trellis controls the sun, and the salt finish on the paving cuts down any glare. (Design: Courtland Paul/Arthur Beggs and Associates)

Houston, Texas

BEFORE: **1.** Lawn **2.** *Quercus virginiana* (Southern live oak) **3.** *Euonymus japonica* **4.** *Pittosporum tobira* 'Variegata'.

Problems: Lawn requires weekly mowing and edging. Euonymus needs spraying for mildew in this area, as well as frequent shearing. Pittosporum requires pruning every month so that lawn can be edged and mowed.

AFTER (lower maintenance): **1.** *Prunus caroliniana* (Carolina cherry laurel) **2.** Southern Indica azaleas **3.** *Buxus microphylla japonica* (Japanese boxwood) **4.** *Quercus virginiana* (Southern live oak) **5.** *Aspidistra elatior* (Cast-iron plant) **6.** *Trachelospermum jasminoides* (Star jasmine).

Solutions: Brick paving eliminates weekly lawn care. Lattice enclosure adds privacy. Star jasmine needs shearing only four times a year, and the aspidistra requires only water. Azaleas need annual feeding and pruning. The cherry laurel obelisks require shearing about every two months. (Design: A. Gregory Catlow)

Milwaukee, Wisconsin

BEFORE: 1. *Ulmus* (Elm) 2. Various flowering shrubs 3. *Juniperus chinensis* 'Pfitzeriana' (Pfitzer juniper) 4. Lawn 5. *Crataegus* (Hawthorn) 6. Forsythia 7. *Hemerocallis* (Daylily) 8. Flagstone with sedum in joints 9. Roses 10. *Cedrus deodara* (Deodar cedar) 11. Lily pool.

Problems: Lawn areas are scattered, making care difficult —especially for those areas on a slope. Many large trees block a lake view and cause shade and root problems in flower beds and lawn. Insufficient room is provided for traffic and outdoor living.

AFTER (lower maintenance): 1. *Stephanandra incisa* 'Crispa' 2. *Crataegus phaenopyrum* (Washington thorn) 3. Existing ash clump 4. *Juniperus chinensis* 'Pfitzeriana' (Pfitzer juniper) 5. *Viburnum lantana* (Wayfaring tree) 6. Existing maple 7. Lawn 8. *Taxus media* (Yew hedge) 9. *Viburnum carlesii* (Korean spice viburnum) 10. *Euonymus fortunei* 'Vegeta' (Big-leaf winter creeper) 11. Gravel mulch 12. *Pachysandra terminalis* (Japanese spurge).

Solutions: One open, sunny, level lawn replaces the scattered and sloping ones. Ample brick surfaces handle traffic and outdoor living. Planting beds are closer to the home for maximum impact and easier care. (Design: Thomas O. Lied)

Freeport, New York

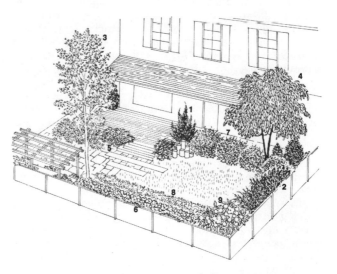

BEFORE: 1. *Betula verrucosa* (European white birch) 2. Azalea 3. *Ilex aquifolium* (English holly) 4. Rhododendron 5. Lawn 6. *Cornus florida* 'Rubra' 7. *Tsuga canadensis* (Canada hemlock) 8. *Ilex cornuta* (Chinese holly).

Problems: Many of the plants used in this garden are not hardy enough for New York winters. The Canada hemlock does not do well in the sandy soil, wind, and ocean salt-spray. Fungus in the lawn is a perpetual problem in the damp atmosphere. The English holly needs regular spraying for leaf miner.

AFTER (lower maintenance): 1. *Juniperus chinensis* 'Torulosa' (Hollywood juniper) 2. *Cotoneaster horizontalis* (Rock cotoneaster) 3. *Betula papyrifera* (Canoe birch, paper birch) 4. *Oxydendron arboreum* (Sorrel tree) 5. *Juniperus sabina* 'Tamariscifolia' (Tamarix juniper) 6. *Ilex glabra* (Inkberry) 7. *Abelia grandiflora* (Glossy abelia) 8. Annuals 9. Rhododendron.

Solutions: Brick paving, timber edging fit in with house design. Pine bark mulch in all planting beds keeps weeds down, temperature even, minimizes water loss. (Design: Rudi Harbauer)

Labor-Saving Techniques

Many of the points discussed in this chapter are re-emphasized throughout the text of the book. These steps toward low maintenance gardening will present many of the possibilities and alternatives as you plan your garden for greater relaxation and less work.

Enjoy your garden and still live a lot

As you are reading through the following suggestions for low maintenance gardening, try to picture your own garden. How can you design and improve it with ease of maintenance as a top priority?

Cast a realistic eye over your garden

Consider from the outset that low *maintenance* gardening can often be high *cost* gardening—at least as far as the initial outlay is concerned. Bricks, lumber, and other paving and building materials can be costly. So can sprinkler systems. Nor do low maintenance gardens sprout up in a day: it takes a year or two of fairly steady watering, for example, to establish a ground cover.

Take a plant inventory of your garden. If you have existing plants, do they suit your needs? They are useful if they give you enjoyment, offer shade or screening, or have other possible advantages. Get rid of a plant if it has no appeal for you and is constantly subject to pests and diseases. Save plants if they have sunk roots deep into the water table; they will be less dependent on your watering.

By spending the time in careful planning, you'll avoid having to constantly change and replant your garden. You can go to work on small sections progressively until your garden is completely redesigned for low maintenance.

Choose simple designs

A simple, free-flowing garden design is the essence of easier maintenance. Avoid frills and scattered plantings—such as isolated flower beds in the middle of the lawn or small groups of perennials in the back of your lot. Instead, concentrate your planting areas and fill them with plants that have similar water, soil, and nutrient requirements.

Pick an informal garden style

An informal garden with smooth, curving lines in which plants grow to their natural shapes is much easier to care for than a formally pruned garden. You won't have to bother so much with the pruning shears and the clippers, and the beauty of the natural growth pattern of many plants won't be spoiled.

Leave the drudgery to others

Try to give your garden a finished and complete look by predominantly using trees and shrubs. Choose specimens for seasonal color so that your garden always has some special point of interest, whether it is a spring flowering plum tree or a pyracantha loaded with brilliant fall berries. This type of garden will not need annuals and bulbs, unless you want a few bright places of concentrated color.

Feel free to ask questions

Many gardening consultants will answer your questions free of charge. Your tax money pays for the advice of your county agricultural agent; look under United States Department of Agriculture in the telephone book. In a number of states, a horticulturist is available for you to speak with on certain days of the week. Call the public service department of the Agricultural Extension Service for the days.

Another good source for garden information is your local nurseryman. He'll be most willing to help you choose your plants and recommend those that grow best in your area. The professional help of a landscape architect, of course, is invaluable in creating an esthetically pleasing low maintenance garden. And don't forget your neighbor or the garden expert on your block. Some of the most valuable information on soil conditions and what grows best in your area will come from next door.

Get a head start in the proper location

Here is a rule that is another of the most important considerations in low maintenance gardening: take the time to find out which plant you should use in the location you have selected. Understand the future requirements of the plant—its sun, water, and soil needs—and also decide what function you want the plant to serve in your

*MESSY OLIVE TREE (left) drops fruit that can stain patio. **Right:** better for low maintenance patio planting is the katsura tree with once-a-year leaf drop, reducing clean-up to an annual affair.*

garden—shade, beauty, food production—before you place it in the garden. Check its size at ultimate growth and give it adequate room to avoid endless pruning. Then plant it correctly in the proper location. There is nothing like a healthy plant, at home with the sun and the soil, to cut down on its maintenance.

Most plants have some low maintenance potential, but all the variables must be considered before the final choice is made. For instance, a bougainvillea against a wall of a house or fence is quite low maintenance, but near a swimming pool it is troublesome. An olive tree in a back hedge row is low maintenance; as a patio tree, it is very dirty and high maintenance.

Check the charts on pages 64-93 for detailed plant recommendations.

Hold the line against nostalgia

Too often, the home gardener has the desire for a low maintenance garden but then ends up placing old favorites in unsuitable sites. For example, although you may cherish azaleas, rhododendrons, and camellias, they will not grow well on a hot, windy hilltop.

Let paving materials give you a hand

Plants are often difficult to grow in the area under the eaves of the house where rain or sprinkler water doesn't reach or in areas under garden benches. These are natural spots for stone or gravel. Stepping stones can easily

STEPPING STONES leading through garden reduce wear on ground cover; add esthetic touch.

be placed throughout the garden for a very attractive effect, such as in ground cover where you often walk. Don't fight the losing battle of trying to grow plants in difficult places; areas where foot traffic is heavy should be paved or covered with non-plant material.

Provide a natural lawn edge to lessen clipping

Lessen clipping chores by creating a natural lawn edge that just dwindles out under trees, shrubs, or merges with ground cover.

Let ground cover hide tree and shrub litter

A loosely textured ground cover—*Vinca major,* Algerian ivy, or St. Johnswort—can be used under shedding trees and shrubs to absorb such fallen material as buds, seeds, blossoms, and leaves. Check with your nurseryman about which ground cover would be most appropriate in your area. The debris from the tree can act as a mulch for the ground cover and a fertilizer for the tree or shrub, consequently eliminating a lot of raking and cleaning for you. This technique is appropriate in a natural-appearing garden.

Banish nuisance plants

You may have plants in your garden that are constantly under attack by every insect in your garden, persistently plagued by disease, or regularly dropping litter all over

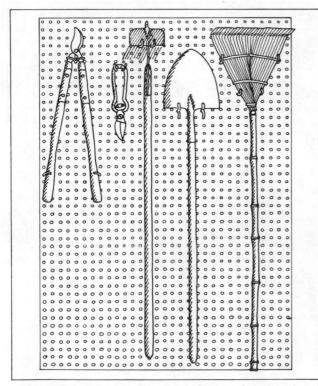

TOOL STORAGE on pegboard cuts down on loss, rust, frazzled nerves; keeps area looking neat.

your patio area. Too often the home gardener feels that he has to live with something just because it happens to be there. He doesn't. A low maintenance garden has to be made up of low maintenance plants, so eliminate any plant that is causing you constant problems and replace it with a less troublesome performer.

Keep track of your tools

Don't spend your gardening time working with improper tools or searching for the proper tool. Trying to cut off a large shrub branch with hand clippers is futile and not consistent with low maintenance gardening; neither is spending valuable time hunting around the garage and yard for a misplaced garden tool. Decide what your garden tool needs are, depending on the size and nature of your garden, and then make sure you have the right tools, stored in a well-organized place. Though you don't need a huge supply of garden tools, you do need the proper tools for the job.

When you are buying garden tools, spend the extra money for the best ones; they will last longer and do the job better and faster.

Keep tools clean and store them in a convenient location so they are always ready when you need them. Keep garden chemicals and amendments in the same area—always out of the reach of children. Your local nursery will often loan or rent you garden equipment, such as fertilizer spreaders or can cutters, that you may not want to buy yourself.

Soil and planting: make it easy on yourself

Two basic gardening skills—the skills of preparing the soil and planting it properly—are extremely important to the low maintenance gardener. Good soil means low maintenance gardening because, set in it, plants will thrive. Such chores as fertilizing and watering will not have to be done so often.

The all-important step: preparing your soil

Consider the following points when the planting season comes around:

Adding soil amendments. In most cases when you start to plant, the soil will need some sort of amendment.

To determine what to add to your soil, you should know whether it is predominantly sandy, loamy, or claylike in composition and what its humus content is. You might compare soil experience with your immediate neighbors to help you determine how plants will perform in your garden soil.

If you want to be more scientific and have your soil chemically analyzed, you will search out exactly what to add to create proper conditions for your plants. You can write to the Agricultural Extension Division of your state university; in some states they will provide you with information about where you can get your soil

GRAVEL under eaves stays in place, looks neat, eliminates hand-watering in places rain doesn't reach.

analyzed. Or you can do it yourself with testing kits advertised in many seed catalogs.

Cultivating. Cultivating temporarily improves the soil by adding air to it and thoroughly mixing into the soil any ingredients you have added. To cultivate in the easiest way possible, choose a good, three-pronged soil cultivator for the small jobs and seriously consider spending a few extra dollars to rent a rotary tiller for the larger jobs.

Drainage. You have a drainage problem if water sits on the surface of the soil and takes a long time to seep through. Plants have a difficult time thriving under these conditions. One solution is to use raised beds or containers filled with ready-made planting mix. Raised beds or containers may have to be watered more often, but if placed so that they blend in with the lines of your garden, they can be an asset. If you feel it necessary to start over again from scratch, hire a landscape architect to design a drainage system for you.

Planting lore

In planning for a lower maintenance garden, you should be aware of several points before you begin selecting plants to set into the soil:

Consider the exposure. Plants must be carefully located for low maintenance. Place shade lovers in the shade, sun lovers in the sun. You may find that if you plant a marigold or other sun-loving plant in a shady area, the plant will shrink instead of growing to its full potential.

Plant at the right time. Take extra effort to check the time of year when a particular plant should be planted.

Occasionally nurseries sell end-of-season plants that would not last long in the garden. Some plants—bulbs, for example—have to be planted in the fall so their roots can become established during cool weather.

Don't go overboard. Check with the nurseryman about the growth limits of a particular plant. Most gardeners tend to overplant initially when plants are small and then in later years must do a great deal of pruning.

Keep clear of overhangs. Avoid planting under wide overhangs. Such areas that immediately skirt the house require hand watering since rain water cannot reach them.

Don't plant in infested soils. Avoid planting in weed or disease-infested soil, especially soil infested with Bermuda grass. Soil should be made weed or disease-free through repeated germination and weed removal or through treatment with a temporary soil sterilant.

Plant towards the end of the day or during cloudy weather. When you are setting out plants in prepared soil, plant them when the hottest part of the day has passed. Since plant materials suffer a certain amount of shock at planting, they are not helped by having to cope with the heat of the sun while they are adjusting to their new environment.

Mulch open areas between plants to control weeds. This is an important labor-saving technique: your plants will have less competition, and you'll have more leisure. (See following section.)

Try placing compatible plants together. Companion planting—the combining of certain plants that benefit each other—is currently receiving much attention. There is some evidence that marigolds, nasturtiums, nicotiana, chives, garlic, basil, savory, feverfew, and many other herbs planted throughout vegetable and flower beds (or in borders around them) help to reduce insect attacks.

Mulching can be magic

What does mulching have to do with low maintenance gardening? Although mulching your garden is a very simple technique, its importance for low maintenance gardening is hard to overemphasize. With mulching, as with proper soil preparation, a little extra time spent in the beginning will save a lot of time throughout the gardening season.

What is a mulch?

A mulch is a layer of material, either organic or inorganic, spread on the soil surface. Organic mulch is applied from 2 to 6 inches deep. Spread in between trees, shrubs, and flower beds, mulch acts as a type of blanket or protective covering for the plant growth. Mulching serves to conserve water for the roots, inhibit weed growth, and— in the case of organic mulches— add humus to the soil.

Mulching is what nature does routinely every year when a tree loses its leaves. Leaves fall and settle at the base of the tree. There they act as a protective covering for the roots of the tree through the winter months. Then the leaves decompose and work their way into the soil to provide the tree with humus and nutrients for new spring growth.

Mulching your way to relaxation

Mulching can certainly cut your garden chores significantly. Some mulching advocates even claim that you can almost eliminate gardening chores by mulching. Let's explore a few of the advantages:

Mulching conserves moisture. It keeps the water in the soil by slowing down evaporation. Your watering chores can be reduced significantly.

Mulching insulates plants. In cold climates, mulching protects plants from winter freezing and thawing conditions that damage plants by heaving them out of the ground, breaking off their finer roots. Mulching will also help to prevent the soil from freezing too deeply.

In warm climates, mulching insulates plants from alternating warm and cold spells to which they may have difficulty adjusting. Freezing conditions may come too early in the fall before the plants are ready; a sudden warming trend may cause the plants to send out new growth that may freeze. Mulches help to prevent this by providing a stable temperature for roots.

Mulching helps to keep weeds down. Weed sprouting is discouraged because the sun cannot get to the weed seedlings to stimulate their growth.

Mulching minimizes erosion. Soil is less apt to be washed away when it is covered by a mulch.

Organic mulching adds humus and nutrients to the soil. This can eliminate the need for you to provide the nutrients. (You *do* need to replace nitrogen in some kinds of organic mulching that do not readily break down; add ammonium sulfate or other nitrogen sources in these cases.)

An array of mulching materials

A great variety of materials can be used as mulches. Since many are by-products of local industries, choose a mulch on the basis of what is readily available in your area and what looks best in your garden. Among the materials you can use are the following organic ones: straw, hay, salt hay (cut from ocean marshes), leaves, hulls from walnuts, peanuts, pecans, buckwheat, ground corn cobs, sugar cane bagasse, shredded bark, wood chips, coffee grounds, pine needles, or any other organic material readily available in your area.

Common inorganic mulches are crushed rock, pebbles, stones, pea gravel, black polyethylene film (which is perforated and usually covered with wood chips or gravel), and thin aluminum strips (more commonly used in vegetable gardens because of their utilitarian look).

You may want to buy or rent a chipper and grind up all of your garden debris, except diseased items, for use as a mulch, avoiding, as a bonus, trips to the dump.

Where should you use a mulch?

Maintenance can be reduced in almost every area in your garden by mulching. Use a permanent mulch, such as gravel or large wood chips, in areas of the garden where you don't plan to replant every year. For flower beds, use a finer, organic mulch that will work its way into the soil and act as a source of humus and nutrients.

Before you mulch, stop and think

The following points are important to consider in order to be successful with mulches:

- Check the source of your mulch so you are not adding a diseased product. For example, sometimes lawn clippings or diseased leaves will reintroduce the disease into the planting area.
- Keep the mulch from covering the crown or the base of the plant.
- If you use peat as a mulch, remember that it can be impermeable to water. When peat moss is dry, water will run off it instead of penetrating through to the soil.
- Because sawdust and ground bark draw nitrogen out of the soil, you will have to add nitrogen if you plan to use these products.

Fertilizing pays generous dividends

You may be asking yourself, "Is fertilizing really necessary for the low maintenance garden? Isn't it only for the dedicated gardener who wants super-green lawn and lush plant growth?" These questions probably stem from your bewilderment at the many types of fertilizers available on the shelves of your local nursery or garden store. You'll see powdered, granular, liquid, complete, balanced, organic, inorganic, special purpose, and many other types of fertilizers. But a relation really does exist between fertilizing and the low maintenance garden. Fertilizing is much more simple than most people think.

For the low maintenance gardener the solution is to buy one all-purpose type of fertilizer and adapt it for various garden needs. Many major chemical companies manufacture complete fertilizers.

Fertilizers for the low-maintenance garden

Choose one or more of the following fertilizers to simplify gardening chores:

Complete, all-purpose fertilizers. These granular types are sold in sacks of various weights. They are mixtures of various ingredients and will always contain a fairly balanced combination of nitrogen, phosphorus, and potassium. Sometimes, they may contain extra ingredients, such as sewage sludge, bonemeal, and iron. A complete fertilizer will satisfy the needs of the majority of your plants and can be applied every four to six weeks throughout the growing season.

Slow-release fertilizers. You only need to apply slow-release fertilizers approximately once a year. The mixture of ingredients in the controlled-release or slow-acting fertilizer has limited solubility in water and is released only as fast as the plant roots can use up the dissolved food. The slow-acting fertilizers are generally more expensive and perhaps a little harder to find, but if you know of a brand name, your nurseryman can tell you where to reach the distributor. Almost all fertilizer manufacturers produce a slow-release product.

The pill. Life has been made easier and more predictable in many areas because of chemistry, and now it can simplify your gardening chores, too. The pill is a blend of synthetic urea and formaldehyde that releases nitrogen very slowly as it breaks down under bacterial action. All you have to do is push the pill into the ground or into the container to the plant's root zone, and its action will last for six months to a year.

Organic sewage sludge fertilizers. Processed and sold by a number of cities, some organic sewage sludge fertilizers, such as Milorganite, are marketed nationally. This organic fertilizer is very popular because it is slow acting and will not burn the plant's roots.

Minimum fertilizing

Fertilizer should usually be applied early in the growing season to stimulate and support new growth. If you apply it just before new growth starts in the spring, plants should have a long growing season. A slow-release fertilizer need only be used once a year or at the beginning of each new growing season. If you are not using a slow-release fertilizer, fertilize every four to six weeks throughout the growing season.

Don't fertilize deciduous trees and shrubs in late summer or fall; fertilizer stimulates new growth, and plants need to become dormant before freezing weather comes. Remember not to over-fertilize to avoid increasing the need for pruning and mowing.

Because of regional differences in growing seasons, you may want to get in touch with your state agricultural extension service or your county agricultural agent for information about appropriate fertilizing times in your region. Remember that agricultural agents are available for both urban and agricultural areas.

The easiest ways to apply fertilizer

Probably the easiest and least complicated way to apply fertilizer is to broadcast it by hand. Simply determine the amount you need, put it in a container, and walk around your yard, tossing evenly.

If you are concerned about even distribution, various gadgets are on the market for broadcasting fertilizer. A hand-operated spreader that whirls out the fertilizer in an even pattern is a popular device; a shoulder-strap version of a hand-operated seeder is another good rig for fertilizing. Either of these devices will save you some time, but if you don't want to bother purchasing one, the hand-broadcasting method will serve the purpose adequately.

If you really want low maintenance fertilizing, it is possible to have fertilizer injected through a sprinkling system. Check with your local dealer about the possibility of attaching such a device to an existing sprinkling system or incorporating it into a new system.

Weeding without tears

Solutions *do* exist for the low maintenance gardener who is trying to eliminate annoying weeds from his garden. Their removal is a necessary garden chore because your garden will be more attractive and healthier without them. Weeds are extremely sturdy plants, often robbing ornamental plants of nutrients, water, and growing space. So it's best to face the fact that if you want a satisfying garden, you have to get rid of weeds.

Forget about studying endless charts of weed killers. Many commercial weed killers are extremely dangerous substances with many undesirable side effects; you can all too easily sterilize the soil and kill off surrounding plant growth.

Attacking garden weeds handily

The easiest way to reduce the weed problem is to apply a 2- to 3-inch layer of mulch over bare garden areas.

DISTRIBUTE *fertilizer four ways:* **Upper left:** *sprinkler system connects to bottle.* **Upper right:** *you hold bottle, hose.* **Lower left:** *spread granules evenly as you walk.* **Lower right:** *use a hopper spreader for the most uniform pattern.*

Unfortunately, you will have to get rid of any existing weeds before putting the mulch down, so get out your hoe or spade and pull the weeds out of the infested area. Keep in mind that, once weeds are pulled, you won't have to be bothered by them again in the area you have worked.

Many people like to use a heavy duty polyethylene film at this point. This plastic film will be added insurance that weeds will not sprout in that area. The film comes in rolls and is quite easy to install. Cut holes in it if shrubs or plants need to come through. It will last for many years, and weeds will find it an impenetrable foe. Air and moisture do not penetrate the film, so keep this in mind if you decide on a spot where you are going to use it. Because the polyethylene film is not particularly attractive in decorative areas of the garden, you will probably want to put a shallow layer of rocks or pebbles on top to hide it.

Refer to the previous section on mulches for the types of material you can use to cover plant beds for reducing weeds. Remember that the mulch should be 2 to 3 inches deep. And while you are mulching your beds, keep in mind the other valuable benefits that a mulch provides for your garden.

Since weeds seldom grow in shady areas or in areas where ground covers have formed a dense growth, you need not be too concerned with weeds in these areas.

Weeds in hard-to-get-at places

Frequently, you'll be bothered by weeds growing through cracks and spaces in walks, driveways, and gravel areas. For these areas, use a lightweight weed oil or a weed oil substitute. Weed oil is relatively safe to use, isn't sticky, and won't permanently stain the surface of the area you are spraying.

Borrow or rent a tank sprayer from a nursery, hold the spray nozzle close to the ground, and thoroughly wet each weed. You won't be sterilizing the soil, and you'll know what you are killing because you directly apply it to the item you want eliminated. The odor is quite strong at first, but it will disappear. Don't spray on windy days. If your area is small and you want to remove the weeds by hand, use a screwdriver that will fit easily

between the cracks to remove the entire weed.

Chemical weed killers

If you have some sort of a specialized problem and oil is not the solution, many specialized weed killers do exist. Read directions *carefully* before applying.

Automate your watering worries away

Dry-season watering is one of the most important single jobs in gardening in the western and arid parts of the United States. It is also one of the most time consuming jobs if not done properly.

Easy watering devices

Depending on how much money you want to invest, your watering chores can be so simplified that you are hardly involved in them at all.

Invest in a good, underground sprinkling system. If you are buying your home, consider that an automatic watering system is one of the best investments you can make. In addition to saving you a lot of work, it will firmly boost the resale value of your home. Your water bills will be less because the most efficient systems use less water than when you water by hand.

Carefully designed and regulated, an automatic system delivers water only as fast as the soil can absorb it, and it distributes water more efficiently and more evenly. Depending on how much money and time you want to invest, you can have your sprinkling system designed and installed professionally—or you can do it yourself.

The cost of automatic sprnkling systems has been greatly reduced because of the use of plastic pipe. This pipe has proved to be very successful, lasting longer than the earlier galvanized, brass, and copper piping. In addition, new sprinkler heads give wider coverage.

Buy an automatic timer and a tensiometer. Two gadgets exist that will save you even more time in your watering

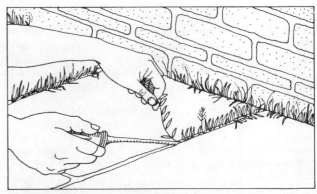

PULL WEED *growing next to plant at an angle, not straight up, to avoid dislodging the plant or damaging its roots.*

REACH FOR *a screwdriver to help you pry stubborn weeds out from between paving blocks, bricks.*

OSCILLATING sprinkler (upper left) eliminates puddles. Upper right: walking sprinkler travels. Lower left: spaghetti system handy for containers. Lower right: Impulse sprinkler directs water.

jobs. If you install a manual watering system, you have reduced the job to going out and turning on the knobs around the yard. You may be watering plants in containers by hand, but that is about all.

If you can spend some extra money, invest in an automatic timer or an automatic sprinkler controller. You set the timer to turn on the garden sprinklers at a specified time—it can go off early in the morning while you are sleeping, or it will automatically turn your sprinkling system on and off while you are away on vacation. These timers are no more difficult to operate than a clock radio or an oven timer. You may need a permit to install the timing system; ask your local building department about codes for installing underground wiring and antisyphon valves (which prevent any water from seeping back into the house water supply).

The second device you can invest in to make your garden watering completely automatic is a moisture indicator, commonly called a tensiometer. This gadget takes the guesswork out of having to decide whether the soil is moist enough or not. Inserted in the ground, it measures the amount of moisture in the soil. When the tensiometer is hooked up to the automatic controls and the soil becomes too dry, the tensiometer will automatically trip the sprinkling system to go off so the soil will reach the desired level of moisture again. Tensiometers will control any type of sprinkling system.

Design your own sprinkler-hose system. If an underground system is impossible for you because of the expense or the fact that you may be renting your home,

you can still simplify your watering chores, making your watering more efficient. A kit is available that contains the parts for you to put sprinkler heads on an ordinary plastic garden hose. Placing the hose in your garden in any pattern you wish, you then install the spray head unit at the spots in the hose that are most advantageous for watering certain areas. A galvanized stake goes into the ground to hold the sprinkler heads upright and to control the position of the hose.

These sprinkler-hose units are also available in ready-made systems of different lengths, with the sprinkler heads and stakes already attached and mounted on a hose. An advantage here is that you can easily move the hose if you don't like the initial coverage. This type of hose could be attached to various faucets around your yard, eliminating the job of dragging hoses all over the yard. With this unit, you can have carefree watering.

Investigate available watering gadgets. Many watering gadgets are on the market that will make watering easier. Browse around and see what fits the needs of your particular situation. Here are a few recommendations:

• *Oscillating sprinklers* are very popular watering devices that distribute the water evenly in a wide, gentle shower. Flooding is seldom a problem. They can be set in different patterns for the area you have to cover —such as a rectangular or square-shaped lawn.
• *Traveling or walking sprinklers* are convenient for lawn areas. They move slowly around the lawn in a set pattern, depending how you program them. These

MOWING STRIP guides wheel of mower, edging tool; helps reduce time and effort of hand clipping.

sprinklers can save hours of labor by eliminating the necessity of dragging and resetting hoses.

- *Spaghetti systems*, developed by nurserymen, are individual tubes reaching to root systems. They can be adapted to home situations for potted plants, trees, and large shrubs. Each plant can get a deep soaking from turning just one valve.
- *Impulse sprinklers*, which are sprinkler heads installed on the periphery of a garden area, shoot water out vigorously and are adjustable according to the area you wish to have covered. These sprinklers, designed for a larger garden area, have sprinkler heads that pop up with water pressure during the watering period. When they are not used, they sink down to ground level.

Follow these simple watering techniques

An awareness of the best watering methods for areas where gardens get little or no rain for months on end will help you to develop plants that are more vigorous.

Deep, thorough, and infrequent watering is the best. It's hard to overstress the importance of slow, deep watering wherever possible, allowing longer intervals between soakings to encourage deep rooting systems. This "feast-famine" watering technique is essential in encouraging plant growth. Deep watering builds sturdy root systems that will withstand such emergencies as sudden heat waves and drought. Shallow watering, on the other hand, keeps roots near the surface where they may dry out and burn.

In general, most plants need about one inch of water per week. If you are not certain about how much water your plants are getting, put a can or a pie tin out and time how long it takes to fill the container to a depth of 1 inch; then you will know how long to water each week. Climatic variations must be considered, of course; if you live in an exceptionally dry or windy area, you will naturally have to water more. If you are in a cool, humid area, plants will require less watering since they transpire less water to the air.

Water early in the morning. Watering at night encourages humid air and mildew; morning watering reduces the incidence or susceptibility of disease. Another reason for watering in the morning is the fact that plants can dry out before the hot sun damages their leaves and tip growth. Plants, like human skin, burn faster when wet. Moreover, when you water early in the day, irrigation water is not reduced by wind and hot, dry air. Water pressure is also best in the morning.

Flooding or soaking is best for shrubs and trees. You don't have to water shrubs and trees as often as you water herbaceous plants, lawns, or plants in containers. A canvas soaker among the shrubs and trees is helpful, allowing the water to soak in slowly and deeply.

Find out the type of soil in your area so you can water according to its needs. If you don't know, ask either your local nurseryman or the county agricultural agent whether you have sandy, loamy, or claylike soil. Different soils have different water capacities. For example, clay soil requires heavier watering because it absorbs slowly and can hold more water. For the same reason, you don't have to water as often. Sandy soil, on the other hand, will not require heavy watering, for water will flow through it much more rapidly. If your soil is sandy, you will use less water but need to apply it more often.

Don't water bare soils. Weeds won't grow as easily without water. Basin watering will help to eliminate weeding between shrubs or trees.

Plant to avoid pests

Preserving and maintaining the ecological balance of the environment plays a very significant role in many aspects of gardening. For this reason, the extensive use of many types of pesticides is no longer practiced. In planning a low maintenance garden, remember that most plants are naturally pest-resistant and may never have to be sprayed. You make extra work for yourself when you plant such pest-attracting plants as modern begonias, roses, strawberries, and cinerarias.

In the 1950s and 1960s, home gardeners had pest-control services spray the entire garden, fence to fence, three or four times a year. By doing this, the ecological balance of the garden was destroyed, and many valuable insect predators were wiped out. Avoid a massive yard spraying; instead, plant with pest-resistant materials.

A light but firm touch with pests

Sometimes a certain organism will feed upon a certain garden plant (even one of the supposedly pest-resistant ones) until you can't stand it. When that happens, here are things you can do:

Spray with water. Remember that many insects can be washed off with water. Preferably in the morning, hose off any plants that have insect problems.

Use a dormant spray. When deciduous plants are completely leafless and when the weather is not freezing, a dormant spray will do much to eliminate the spring crop of scale insects, aphids, lichens, and algae. Spray only when it's not raining, when the temperature is above freezing, and when there is no wind.

If you think a dormant spray will help certain plants in your garden, you can buy a ready-made dormant spray mix in your garden store or hire a commercial spraying service to do the spraying. Only spray the plants or trees on which you have any special insect or disease problems. Roses, peaches, and nectarines are plants that often benefit from a dormant spray.

Apply a chemical as a last resort. When a valuable plant is obviously in danger of losing its life or its entire annual crop from the action of a certain organism, buy whatever product is currently believed to control that organism. Read the product's label carefully. Then apply it only as instructed.

The path to lighthearted pruning

Like watering your garden, pruning can be an enormous garden chore if you let it be. However, good solutions do exist to make pruning compatible with low maintenance gardening. You really don't need to be out with the machete hacking away at the excess growth in your yard.

Minimizing future pruning chores

What does landscape planning have to do with pruning? The answer is that a carefully planned landscape can eliminate most pruning chores—an important part of the answer to low maintenance gardening.

Plants should be properly spaced in the landscape so that they can develop their full potential of beauty—their growth habit, flowers, berries, or whatever prized characteristics they may possess. When you choose plants for your new landscape, be certain to check carefully with your nurseryman before buying a particular plant to see what its ultimate size will be. Keep in mind these points:

- Check future height and width of a plant carefully, considering what the plant will look like in five to eight years.
- Space plants according to mature height and spread.
- Fill in with temporary plantings of annuals, bulbs, or ground cover if you think the landscape looks too sparse.

Watch out for some common pitfalls. Proper placement of plants is extremely important in a low maintenance garden. Consider the following directions carefully:

- Resist the urge to place tall-growing plants in front of windows so that they will always have to be cut back.
- Be selective in what you plant under an overhang. Don't get trapped into having to trim frequently in order to prevent a shrub or tree from filling in under the overhang.
- Choose your entryway plant carefully so it will not grow to constantly block the front walk.

Easing present pruning chores

The low maintenance gardener could consider this a basic rule concerning pruning: if there is a plant in the garden that constantly has to be pruned or cut back, get rid of it. Study your complete landscape and decide which plants are too crowded together. Possibly the previous owner zealously filled up the whole landscape with small trees and shrubs without considering their ultimate size. You may have to remove several plants or shrubs at intervals. Decide which hardy plants you like best and leave them. Get rid of others that are crowding your garden. By doing this, you will have a much more attractive landscaping pattern, virtually eliminating a lot of your pruning.

Pruning the low maintenance garden

To arrange for the least amount of necessary pruning, keep this idea in mind:

Try a once-a-year pruning approach. If you have spaced your plants properly, all you'll need to do is cut out any dead or damaged wood once a year, shaping up any plants where they need it. In general, prune in late winter or early spring after frost danger has passed. With deciduous plants, you can easily see what branches need to be removed before they leaf out. If you wait until summer for major pruning efforts, there may not be enough time for plants to bud and bloom. You may find that light pruning or pinching back during the summer may be beneficial in order to prevent new growth that would later need pruning. Keep in mind another general rule about pruning: prune after flowering.

The bare basics of pruning

Since the basic facts of pruning are important but simple, you can do a good job with any plant knowing these few techniques:

- If you want bushier growth, pinch the terminal bud to direct growth outward rather than upward.
- If you want to thin a plant, prune new growth between established branches at intervals along a trunk.
- Cut right above a growing bud.

If you have to prune to shape a plant, stand back away from the plant, study its growth habit, and then prune as artistically as possible to retain the basic beauty of the plant's form. Keep standing back and observing intermittently while you prune. Refer to Sunset's *Pruning Handbook* for any questions you may have about individual plants.

Plants that Take Minimum Care

Essential for the aspiring low maintenance gardener is a knowledge of which plant materials thrive with least care in his area.

The following text and charts include materials you may want to use: trees, shrubs, ground covers, vines, perennials, and bulbs. Plant materials have been listed alphabetically by botanical name in charts. You can select those that are most probably right for your area by noting their zone numbers in the chart and then checking these against the eight zones in the United States Department of Agriculture Plant Hardiness Zone Map reproduced below.

Doing this will give you a fairly accurate estimate of which plants will tolerate the freezing level in your region. But, of course, temperature level is not your only concern in selecting plants. Plant hardiness is also governed by special soil requirements, humidity level, elevation, sudden temperature change, and exposure. These factors often create micro-climates—even in as small an area as your own garden.

Because of this, the Plant Hardiness Zone Map should only be approached as a general guide. The only *truly* accurate Plant Hardiness Zone Map would be one that was the size of the United States itself.

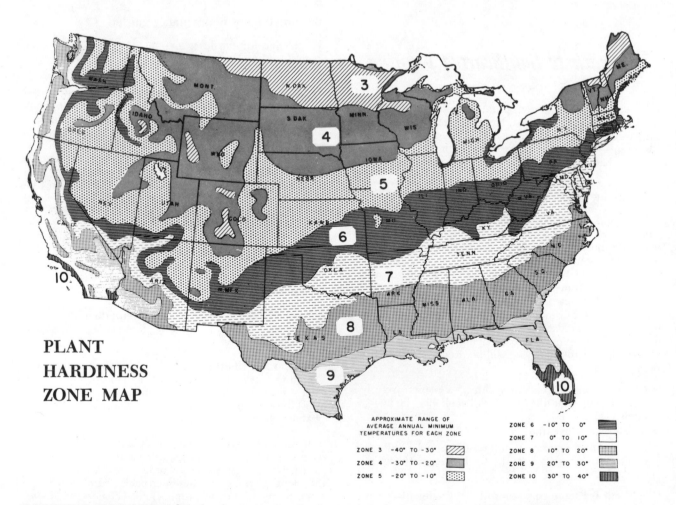

PLANT HARDINESS ZONE MAP

APPROXIMATE RANGE OF AVERAGE ANNUAL MINIMUM TEMPERATURES FOR EACH ZONE	
ZONE 3	−40° TO −30°
ZONE 4	−30° TO −20°
ZONE 5	−20° TO −10°
ZONE 6	−10° TO 0°
ZONE 7	0° TO 10°
ZONE 8	10° TO 20°
ZONE 9	20° TO 30°
ZONE 10	30° TO 40°

HARDINESS ZONE MAP *is based only on freezing levels. Refer to plant charts (pages 62–93) for further information about plant needs. These may vary throughout a zone. (Note: zones 1 and 2 are mainly in Canada.)*

Trees...
the gardener's best friend

Can you imagine any landscape without trees? The starkness of the terrain would be immediately evident. So often, we take a tree for granted and then complain about having to rake up after it in the fall. But, in fact, trees are the backbone of the landscape for community and home. If well chosen, trees require less maintenance than any plant in your garden.

Questions to ask about trees

You should be very hard-hearted about choosing low maintenance trees for your garden. Ask the following questions before you ultimately decide on a tree:

Do you want a deciduous or nondeciduous tree? Most people interested in low maintenance gardens will automatically assume that they want a nondeciduous tree so they won't have to rake up after it in the fall. But you really should consider a few other things before automatically deciding on a nondeciduous tree. First, consider its function. If you want shade in the summer and light in the winter, perhaps you want a deciduous tree. Second, consider that nondeciduous trees, such as magnolias and loquats, shed leaves all year round. Third, take into account that some deciduous trees are very easy to clean up after. The fruitless mulberry, maple, and ginkgo change colors and then drop their leaves all at once, so you have to rake up only once or twice in the fall.

What purpose do you want the tree to serve? If you force yourself to define the purpose of the tree, it will help you in choosing the right one. Among the possible functions of a tree or a group of trees would be to provide shade, privacy, beauty, or to act as a windbreak, a screen, a screen against traffic noise, or fruit bearer.

What size and shape is most appropriate for the function of the tree? Depending on the function you have decided you want the tree to serve, decide how large and what shape you need. If you desire a shade tree, you will want one with a rounded or umbrella-shaped top, such as a Modesto ash or a camphor tree. If you want a windbreak, you may need a columnar tree with tightly knitted limbs or branches, such as an Italian cypress. (Always check first to see if any of the trees recommended is suitable for your area.)

Be very careful about the ultimate size of the tree. Future growth is very frequently overlooked, and it is absolutely paramount that the size specification for a tree be set before any other factor is considered. Since a tree dominates all other plant types in the garden, most home gardens should use only two, three, or four trees.

If you plant too many, the rest of the garden suffers—and so does the gardener.

Does the tree drop excessive litter? Do a little research in a good gardening encyclopedia or ask your nurseryman what materials fall from the tree during the cycle of a year. Does it drop fruit, seedpods, sap, flowers, twigs, or nuts? Buy carefully and purchase from a reliable nursery source. Distinctions are often rather fine. For example, the male *Ginkgo biloba* tree is one of the highest recommended low maintenance trees throughout the United States. But you must be careful that you get a male tree, for each fall the female tree sheds a quantity of foul-smelling fruit. Olive trees drop loads of juicy, purple olives that children inevitably track into the house; a Chinese wingnut tree can clog sewer lines with its aggressive roots.

Where are you going to place the tree? Where you place a tree is an important factor in its maintenance. As a good example, Lombardy poplars are definitely not low maintenance on the edge of a driveway, but if you have a larger piece of property and plant them towards the rear of the property where they have plenty of room to expand, they are fine. Similarly, an olive tree located in an area of the garden away from the traffic pattern is splendid, but in a patio area or entry walk, an olive tree is a nuisance. Watch purpose and placement.

How long will the tree live? Some varieties of fruit trees and flowering, decorative fruit trees don't last longer than 10 to 15 years. Then they have to be removed and replaced—a big chore. Another tree, such as tulip tree, will live through many generations of home owners in its neighborhood. For a low maintenance garden, choose a long-lived tree.

Are suckering or self-seeding problems? Some trees send out so many suckers or seeds that you spend a great amount of time trying to prevent the offspring from taking over your yard. The Norway maple and the black locust trees are noted for suckering and self-seeding. Be certain to check this before you buy a tree. Check also to see whether or not the tree may have invasive roots which could clog sewage systems—poplars are notorious for doing this.

Is the tree sturdy, or could it blow over or break off easily in a storm? A few kinds of trees are noticeably brittle and therefore susceptible to branch-breaking in storms. At the top of this list are the leguminous trees (whose fruits look like big bean pods). Double-check with your nurseryman about the brittleness of the tree you choose.

(Turn page for Trees chart)

Small Trees (About 20 ft.)

NAME	HARDINESS ZONES	EVERGREEN OR DECIDUOUS	HEIGHT	COMMENTS
ACACIA baileyana BAILEY ACACIA	9-10	E	To 20-40 ft.	One of hardiest acacias. Good on banks as a multi-trunked tree-shrub.
ACER circinatum VINE MAPLE	3-9	D	To 5-35 ft.	Vinelike in forest shade, upright tree in full sun. Blazing fall color.
A. ginnala AMUR MAPLE	3-7	D	To 20 ft.	Red fall color. Neat shape, minimum litter, few pests.
A. palmatum JAPANESE MAPLE	6-10	D	To 20 ft.	Most airy and delicate maple. Slow-growing. Best in filtered shade.
ALOE arborescens TREE ALOE	8-10	E	To 15-18 ft.	Succulent with spiny leaves, showy winter bloom. Stands drought. Sun or shade.
AMELANCHIER canadensis SHADBLOW, SERVICE BERRY	3-9	D	To 30 ft.	Showy, spring flowers, red fruits, fall color. Roots not invasive. Casts light shade.
CORNUS florida FLOWERING DOGWOOD, EASTERN DOGWOOD	6-9	D	To 20 ft.	Profuse spring bloom, brilliant red fall berries, leaf color. Many varieties.
C. mas CORNELIAN CHERRY	4-7	D	To 15-20 ft.	One of earliest dogwoods to bloom. Withstands subzero temperatures.
CRATAEGUS phaenopyrum WASHINGTON THORN	5-9	D	To 25 ft.	Shiny red fruits in autumn last through winter. Least susceptible hawthorn to fireblight.
CUPRESSOCYPARIS leylandii HYBRID CYPRESS	7-10	E	To 15-20 ft.	Extremely fast growth. Narrow, pyramidal form. Accepts wide variety of soils and climates.
DRACAENA fragrans	9-10	E	To 20 ft.	Palmlike leaves. Slow growing.
ELAEAGNUS angustifolia RUSSIAN OLIVE	3-9	D	To 20 ft.	Fast growing, drought resistant. Best in cold winter, hot summer climates.
ERIOBOTRYA japonica LOQUAT	7-10	E	To 15-30 ft.	Big, leathery leaves, sweet fruits. Best with ample water, tolerates drought when established.
HALESIA carolina CAROLINA SILVER BELL, SNOWDROP TREE	5-9	D	To 20-30 ft.	White spring flower clusters, interesting winter fruits. Bushy if not pruned when young.
HETEROMELES arbutifolia TOYON, CHRISTMAS BERRY, CALIFORNIA HOLLY	7-10*	E	To 15-25 ft.	Multiple-trunked. Bright red winter berries. Drought tolerant.
ILEX pendunculosa HOLLY	6-10	E	To 15 ft.	Bright red berries.
LIVISTONA chinensis CHINESE FOUNTAIN PALM	9-10	E	To 15 ft.	Very slow growing. Leaves have a pronounced droop.
MAGNOLIA stellata STAR MAGNOLIA	5-10	D	To 10-20 ft.	Profuse, early bloom.
M. soulangiana SAUCER MAGNOLIA	5-10	D	To 25 ft.	Huge flowers bloom before leaves expand.
MALUS scheideckeri SCHEIDECKER CRABAPPLE	3-9	D	To 20 ft.	Dense tree with semi-double, rose-pink flowers. Small yellow fruit through November.
OXYDENDRUM arboreum SOURWOOD, SORREL TREE	5-9	D	To 15-40 ft.	Fall, spring leaf color, summer flowers. Requires acid soil, ample water.

Except Zone 7 in East

NAME	HARDINESS ZONES	EVERGREEN OR DECIDUOUS	HEIGHT	COMMENTS
PINUS aristata BRISTLECONE PINE	5-8	E	To 20 ft.	Very slow growing. Often heavy-trunked.
P. cembroides MEXICAN PINON PINE	6-10	E	To 10-25 ft.	Stout, spreading branches. Drought resistant.
PRUNUS ilicifolia HOLLYLEAF CHERRY	8-10	E	To 20-30 ft.	Usually broader than high. Contrasting new and old foliage.
P. lusitanica PORTUGAL LAUREL	7-10	E	To 10-20 ft.	Spring bloom, red summer fruit. Multi-trunked.
P. serrulata JAPANESE FLOWERING CHERRY	6-9	D	To 20 ft.	Many varieties with white or pink flowers.
PYRUS calleryana	5-9	D	To 15-45 ft.	Red fall foliage, early white bloom.
P. kawakamii EVERGREEN PEAR	8-10	E - D	To 20-30 ft.	Sprawling habit, makes good espalier. Fruit inedible.
RHAPIS humilis SLENDER LADY PALM	9-10	E	To 18 ft.	Very slow growing. Fan-shaped palm, grows in clumps. Takes shade.
RHUS glabra SMOOTH SUMAC	4-8	D	To 10-20 ft.	Scarlet fall foliage, scarlet fruits. Takes extreme heat and cold, all soils but the most alkaline.

Medium Trees (About 20-40 ft.)

NAME	HARDINESS ZONES	EVERGREEN OR DECIDUOUS	HEIGHT	COMMENTS
ALBIZIA julibrissin SILK TREE	7-10	D	To 40 ft.	Pink fluffy flowers on ferny-leafed branches. Best in high summer heat. Some litter. Rapid growth.
AMELANCHIER laevis SHADBUSH	3-8	D	To 30-35 ft.	Purplish young foliage, roots not invasive.
BETULA verrucosa EUROPEAN WHITE BIRCH	4-10	D	To 30-40 ft.	Delicate, lacy. Not for patio or parking areas because of tendency to attract aphids that drip honeydew.
CERCIDIUM floridum BLUE PALO VERDE	8-10	D	To 25 ft.	Will survive much drought but produces lusher growth with water.
CERCIS canadensis EASTERN REDBUD	5-10	D	To 25-35 ft.	Pink flowers in early spring. Fall color.
CRATAEGUS crus-galli	5-9	D	To 36 ft.	Glossy leaves, bright fall color.
C. mollis DOWNY HAWTHORN	5-9	D	To 30 ft.	Larger than most fruiting hawthorns.
CUPANIOPSIS anacardioides CARROT WOOD, TUCKEROO	9-10	D	To 30 ft.	Creates heavy shade. Tolerates poor drainage.

NAME	HARDINESS ZONES	EVERGREEN OR DECIDUOUS	HEIGHT	COMMENTS
FRANKLINIA alatamaha	6-9	D	To 20-30 ft.	Bright, spoon-shaped leaves turn scarlet in autumn. White, late summer bloom. Needs rich, light, acid soil; ample water.
FRAXINUS pennsylvanica GREEN ASH	2-7	D	To 30-40 ft.	Compact, oval crown. Takes wet soil, severe cold.
F. velutina ARIZONA ASH	6-9	D	To 25-30 ft.	Withstands hot, dry conditions and cold down to −10°. Pyramidal when young, more open when mature. Slow growing.
HYMENOSPORUM flavum SWEETSHADE	9-10	E	To 20-40 ft.	Attractive trees, don't need staking in groves.
JACARANDA acutifolia	9-10	D-E	To 25-40 ft.	Often multi-trunked. Fernlike leaves drop February-March, usually return quickly. Lavender summer bloom.
KOELREUTERIA paniculata GOLDENRAIN TREE	6-8	D	To 20-35 ft.	Yellow summer flower clusters. Takes cold, heat, drought, wind, alkaline soil.
LAURUS nobilis SWEET BAY, GRECIAN LAUREL	8-10	E	To 12-40 ft.	Compact, often multi-trunked. The traditional bay leaf of cookery.
MAGNOLIA denudata YULAN MAGNOLIA	5-10	D	To 35 ft.	White, fragrant flowers.
MALUS floribunda JAPANESE FLOWERING CRABAPPLE	3-9	D	To 20-30 ft.	Pink, white, or red flowers and showy fruit. Hardy, tolerant of wet soil.
M. ioensis plena BECHTEL CRABAPPLE	3-10	D	To 25 ft.	Large, pink, fragrant flowers.
MELALEUCA quinquenervia CAJEPUT TREE	5-10	E	To 20-40 ft.	Summer and fall flowers. Can take much or little water.
MORUS alba 'fruitless' FRUITLESS MULBERRY	5-9	D	To 35 ft.	Rapid growth in hot climates and alkaline soils.
OLEA europaea COMMON OLIVE	9-10	E	To 25-30 ft.	Soft, willowlike foliage, gnarled trunk in maturity. Thrives in hot, dry summers; moist soils. Plant where fruit drop not a problem.
PINUS contorta SHORE PINE, BEACH PINE	4-10*	E	To 20-35 ft.	Irregular shape. Hardy anywhere but not best in dry, hot areas.
P. nigra AUSTRIAN PINE	4-7	E	To 40-60 ft.	Dense, stout pyramid; good windbreak. Adapts to winter cold and wind.
PROSOPIS glandulosa torreyana MESQUITE	9-10	E	To 30 ft.	Wide-spreading shade tree. Tolerates drought, alkaline soils, or irrigated lawns. Best in deep soil.
PRUNUS cerasifera 'Thundercloud' FLOWERING PURPLE-LEAF PLUM	5-10	D	To 20 ft.	Dark coppery leaves. Light pink to white flowers.
P. subhirtella autumnalis AUTUMN FLOWERING CHERRY	5-9	D	To 25-30 ft.	Spring and fall bloom.
QUERCUS texana TEXAS OAK	9-10**	E	To 35 ft.	Good shade tree.
RHUS lancea AFRICAN SUMAC	9-10	E	To 25 ft.	Airy tree with dark red, rough bark, interesting branch pattern. Slow growing. Tolerates high summer heat, drought.
R. typhina STAGHORN SUMAC	3-9	D	To 15-30 ft.	Bright fall color, flower clusters in June, crimson fruits last all winter. Takes extreme heat and cold.

Except in East
**Except Zone 10 in West*

NAME	HARDINESS ZONES	EVERGREEN OR DECIDUOUS	HEIGHT	COMMENTS
SALIX babylonica WEEPING WILLOW	7-10	D	To 30-50 ft.	Very fast growing. Needs lots of water; tolerates poor drainage.
SOPHORA japonica JAPANESE PAGODA TREE, CHINESE SCHOLAR TREE	5-9	D	To 20-60 ft.	Good spreading shade tree but not where seeds, pods could stain. Not fussy as to soil, water.
SORBUS aucuparia EUROPEAN MOUNTAIN ASH	4-8	D	To 20-30 ft.	Late spring bloom, berrylike fruit. Some litter.
STYRAX japonica JAPANESE SNOWDROP TREE	7-9	D	To 30 ft.	White, fragrant June flowers. Thrives with plenty of water, good drainage.
TILIA cordata LITTLELEAF LINDEN	4-8	D	To 30-50 ft.	Dense, pyramidal form. Fragrant July bloom.

Large Trees (Over 40 ft.)

NAME	HARDINESS ZONES	EVERGREEN OR DECIDUOUS	HEIGHT	COMMENTS
ABIES concolor WHITE FIR	5-9	E	To 120 ft.	One of the best firs for landscape use. Thrives in moist climates. Bluish-green foliage.
ACER platanoides NORWAY MAPLE	4-8	D	To 50-80 ft.	Dense foliage. Many purple-leafed forms. Adapts to many soil, climate conditions. Voracious root system, honey drip from aphids a problem.
A. rubrum SCARLET, RED MAPLE	3-9	D	To 40-90 ft.	Fairly fast growth; red leaves, flowers, fruits. Suited to sandy and poorly drained soils.
A. saccharum SUGAR MAPLE	4-8	D	To 60-90 ft.	Spectacular fall color in cold winter areas.
BETULA nigra RIVER BIRCH, RED BIRCH	4-10	D	To 50-90 ft.	Fast growing when young, then slows. Pyramidal form. Needs ample water.
CALOCEDRUS decurrens INCENSE CEDAR	6-10	E	To 75-90 ft.	Slow growing at first, then fast. Deep, infrequent watering in youth makes mature tree unusually drought tolerant.
CEDRUS atlantica ATLAS CEDAR	7-10	E	To 60 ft.	Slow to moderate growing conifer. Little or no pruning.
C. deodara DEODAR CEDAR	7-10	E	To 80 ft.	Graceful conifer with a 40 ft. spread at ground level. Fast growing. Almost no care.
CELTIS occidentalis COMMON HACKBERRY	4-9	D	To 50 ft.	Deep rooting; no surface roots to break pavement or lawn. When established takes heat, wind, drought, alkaline soil.
CERCIDIPHYLLUM japonicum KATSURA TREE	5-8	D	To 40-75 ft.	Light, dainty branch and leaf pattern; shows tints of red. Needs protection from hot sun, dry winds.
CORNUS nuttallii PACIFIC DOGWOOD, WESTERN DOGWOOD	7-9*	D	To 50 ft.	One or several trunks. Spring and often fall bloom; red fall fruits. Needs good drainage, infrequent summer watering. 'Goldspot' has leaves splashed with yellow.
CRYPTOMERIA japonica JAPANESE CRYPTOMERIA	7-9	E	To 150 ft.	Graceful conifer. Many smaller varieties. *C.j.* 'Elegans' turns reddish in winter.

Except in East

NAME	HARDINESS ZONES	EVERGREEN OR DECIDUOUS	HEIGHT	COMMENTS
EUCALYPTUS polyanthemos SILVER DOLLAR GUM	9-10*	E	To 20-60 ft.	Round and lance-shaped leaves. Drought tolerant; pest free. Grows almost anywhere except wet places.
E. sideroxylon RED IRONBARK, PINK IRONBARK	9-10*	E	To 20-80 ft.	Fast growing, drought tolerant. Avoid wet adobe soils.
FAGUS sylvatica 'Pendula' WEEPING BEECH	5-9	D	To 90 ft.	Needs space to spread out. Branches touch the ground.
FRAXINUS americana WHITE ASH	3-8	D	To 80 ft.	Pyramidal shape; purplish fall color.
F. uhdei EVERGREEN ASH, SHAMEL ASH	9-10	D-E	To 70-80 ft.	Evergreen in mild areas; loses leaves in cold climates. Fast growing, narrow when young, spreads with age.
F. velutina 'Modesto' MODESTO ASH	6-9	D	To 50 ft.	Bright yellow fall color. Prune for strong framework to withstand wind.
GINKGO biloba MAIDENHAIR TREE	5-10	D	To 50-90 ft.	Graceful, fan-shaped leaves turn gold in fall. Plant only male trees; female has messy, bad-smelling fruits.
GLEDITSIA triacanthos inermis HONEY LOCUST	5-9	D	To 35-70 ft.	Hardy to cold, heat, wind, some drought. Best in cold winters, hot summers. Thornless, few or no pods.
GYMNOCLADUS dioica KENTUCKY COFFEE TREE	5-9	D	To 50 ft.	Picturesque tree in winter. Takes some drought, much heat, cold, poor soil when established. Male tree is fruitless.
JUNIPERUS virginiana RED CEDAR	3-9	E	To 50-90 ft.	Conical shape, red winter color. Hardiest of tree junipers.
LIQUIDAMBAR styraciflua AMERICAN SWEET GUM	7-10	D	To 60-80 ft.	Brilliant fall foliage. Upright, cone-shaped.
LIRIODENDRON tulipifera TULIP TREE	6-10	D	To 60-80 ft.	Pyramidal-shaped crown. Bright yellow fall color. Tulip-shaped flowers on mature tree. Needs deep, rich, well-drained soil.
MAGNOLIA grandiflora SOUTHERN MAGNOLIA, BULL BAY	7-10	E	To 80 ft.	Big leathery leaves; large white, fragrant flowers.
MALUS baccata SIBERIAN CRABAPPLE	3-10	D	To 50 ft.	One of the tallest and hardiest crabapples. White flowers; red and yellow fruits.
MAYTENUS boaria MAYTEN TREE	8-10	E	To 30-50 ft.	Long, pendulous branches have grace of a weeping willow but tree is neater, lacks invasive roots. Needs good drainage.
PELTOPHORUM dubium	10	E	To 50 ft.	Fernlike, tropical appearance.
PHELLODENDRON amurense AMUR CORK TREE	3-8	D	To 30-45 ft.	Handsome in winter with corky bark. Takes high summer heat, deep winter cold.
PICEA pungens COLORADO SPRUCE	3-7	E	To 80-100 ft.	Stiff, horizontal branches form a broad pyramid. Bluish foliage.
PINUS banksiana JACK PINE	3-8	E	To 75 ft.	Grows on banks, in dry areas where nothing else will.
P. canariensis CANARY ISLAND PINE	9-10	E	To 60-80 ft.	Fast growing, drought tolerant. Has a slender pyramid when young, a round crown when mature.
P. flexilis LIMBER PINE	2-7	E	To 45-75 ft.	Very slow growing. Often flat-topped in maturity.
P. halepensis ALEPPO PINE	8-10	E	To 30-60 ft.	Formal, cone-shaped. Takes heat, drought, wind, poor soils, down to 0° when established.

Except in East

LEFT: Heteromeles arbutifolia *(Toyon) features red winter berries.* **Center:** Ginkgo biloba *(Maidenhair tree) displays yellow fall foliage.* **Right:** Cedrus deodara *(Deodar cedar) is fast growing.*

NAME	HARDINESS ZONES	EVERGREEN OR DECIDUOUS	HEIGHT	COMMENTS
P. pinea ITALIAN STONE PINE	8-10	E	To 40-80 ft.	Grows from a globe to flat-topped form. Takes heat and drought when established.
P. strobus WHITE PINE	3-8	E	To 100 ft.	Fine-textured; handsome in form, color. Slow growing as seedling, then fast.
P. sylvestris SCOTCH PINE	3-8	E	To 70-100 ft.	Full pyramid in youth, irregular with age. Often turns red-brown in cold winters, but recovers.
P. taeda LOBLOLLY PINE	7-10	E	To 90-165 ft.	Native to eastern coast of U.S.
P. thunbergiana JAPANESE BLACK PINE	4-10	E	To 20-100 ft.	Takes to pruning in youth; excellent in containers.
PISTACIA chinensis CHINESE PISTACHE	8-10	D	To 40-60 ft.	Bright fall color; only scarlet-turning tree in desert. Takes any soil or amount of water.
PLATANUS acerifolia LONDON PLANE TREE	5-10	D	To 40-80 ft.	Fast growing; tolerates most soils.
PODOCARPUS gracilior FERN PINE	9-10	E	To 60 ft.	Slow growing. Heavy, graceful foliage often needs staking. Needs some shade where hot.
POPULUS sargentii WESTERN COTTONWOOD	4-9	D	To 90 ft.	Rapid growth. Best in cold winter, hot summer areas. Not for small gardens
P. tremuloides QUAKING ASPEN	3-7	D	To 60 ft.	Dainty, fluttering leaves, brilliant yellow fall color. Best at high elevations.
PRUNUS americana AMERICAN PLUM	4-8	D	To 50 ft.	Profuse, spring bloom, willowlike leaves.

NAME	HARDINESS ZONES	EVERGREEN OR DECIDUOUS	HEIGHT	COMMENTS
P. padus EUROPEAN BIRD CHERRY	3-8	D	To 45 ft.	Good foliage, fruit, bloom. 'Plena' has double flowers.
P. sargentii SARGENT CHERRY	5-8	D	To 75 ft.	Deep pink bloom, scarlet autumn foliage.
PYRUS calleryana 'Bradford' ORNAMENTAL BRADFORD PEAR	5-9	D	To 50 ft.	Red fall foliage; inedible fruit. Resists wind damage, grows well in most soils.
QUERCUS agrifolia COAST LIVE OAK	9-10*	E	To 20-70 ft.	Wide-spreading. Hollylike leaves. Greedy roots.
Q. chrysolepis CANYON LIVE OAK	9-10*	E	To 20-60 ft.	Whitish bark; handsome round-headed or spreading form.
Q. coccinea SCARLET OAK	4-9	D	To 60-80 ft.	High, open-branching habit. Leaves turn bright scarlet in cold autumns. Fine to garden under.
Q. laurifolia LAUREL OAK	9-10**	D-E	To 60 ft.	'Darlington' more compact, keeps its leaves longer than other species.
Q. macrocarpa BUR OAK, MOSSY CUP OAK	4-10	D	To 60-75 ft.	Rugged looking. Tolerates adverse conditions.
Q. nigra WATER OAK	7-10	D-E	To 75 ft.	Conical to round top, small leaves. Thrives in wet sites.
Q. palustris PIN OAK	5-9	D	To 50-80 ft.	Pyramidal form when young, round-headed at maturity, branches droop to ground. Needs good drainage.
Q. rubra RED OAK	4-8	D	To 90 ft.	New leaves red in spring, brownish-orange in fall. Needs fertile soil, plenty of water. Deep roots.
Q. virginiana SOUTHERN LIVE OAK	8-10	D-E	To 60 ft.	Wide crown with heavy limbs. Deciduous in cold winters. Thrives in rich soil, ample water.
SEQUOIA sempervirens COAST REDWOOD	8-10	E	To 70-90 ft.	Fast growing; natives surpass 350 ft. Fresh and woodsy smelling. Likes plenty of water.
TAXODIUM distichum BALD CYPRESS	5-10	D	To 100 ft.	Delicate foliage sprays. Pyramidal in youth, broad-topped in age. Any soil but alkaline. Takes wet or dry conditions.
THUJA occidentalis AMERICAN ARBORVITAE	3-8	E	To 40-60 ft.	Many smaller varieties. Needs moisture to look its best.
T. plicata WESTERN RED CEDAR	5-9	E	To 200 ft.	Graceful sprays, broad spread on lower branches. Takes wet conditions.
TILIA americana AMERICAN LINDEN, BASSWOOD	4-8	D	To 40-60 ft.	Compact, narrow crown; fragrant summer flowers.
TSUGA canadensis CANADA HEMLOCK	3-8	E	To 90 ft.	Dense, pyramidal form, graceful branches. Good lawn tree.
T. caroliniana CAROLINA HEMLOCK	5-8	E	To 75 ft.	Soft appearance, nice specimen.
T. heterophylla WESTERN HEMLOCK	4-8*	E	To 125-200 ft.	Thrives in moist mountain atmosphere. Fernlike foliage, picturesque conifer.
T. mertensiana MOUNTAIN HEMLOCK	3-8*	E	To 50-90 ft.	Much smaller in home gardens. Tufty looking branches. Good for containers.
ULMUS americana AMERICAN ELM	3-9*	E	To 100 ft.	For out-of-the-way places where suckers no problem.

Except in Midwest, East
**Except Zone 10 in West*

NAME	HARDINESS ZONES	EVERGREEN OR DECIDUOUS	HEIGHT	COMMENTS
U. parvifolia CHINESE EVERGREEN ELM	8-10	E-D	To 40-60 ft.	Very fast growth; wide spread.
WASHINGTONIA robusta MEXICAN FAN PALM	9-10	E	To 100 ft.	Very fast growing. Tall, slender trunk, compact crown.
ZELKOVA serrata SAWLEAF ZELKOVA	5-10	D	To 60 ft.	Leaves similar to elm; very pest-free.

Shrubs...
they fill many needs

Shrubs, like trees, provide privacy in garden areas by screening certain areas and acting as boundaries. In addition, shrubs soften the lines of house by blending the house into the landscape. Available in all shapes, sizes, colors, textures, and forms, shrubs give the garden great variety and the feeling of airiness and lightness.

Questions to ask about shrubs

Be thorough in selecting shrubs so that the ones you choose might be low maintenance in your garden:

How tall and wide will the shrub be at maturity? The biggest maintenance problem with shrubs is the pruning they require when they are spaced too closely together or planted in the wrong place. A shrub grouping of xylosma is very effective as a screen and for adding softness to a garden area, but if it is not given adequate and generous space, you'll have to constantly trim and cut them back. Another common mistake is placing a shrub such as the podocarpus (a tall, narrow landscaping shrub) under the eaves of a house. This shrub is always pushing up against the eaves and has to be constantly pruned back. Shrubs look better if they are allowed to grow naturally with only minimal pruning, cutting out dead wood, or shaping.

Take the time to plan your shrub areas. Shrubs need to have light penetration and air circulation in order to grow well. Poor placement can cause mildew, dying out, or the need for excessive pruning for plant control.

What is the function of the shrub and where should it be placed? Shrubs provide privacy and beauty. They also act as windbreaks and screens. Decide what purpose you want a shrub to serve.

If you spot shrubs all around your garden, you will have increased maintenance caring for them. You'll have to mow and trim around them if they are spread throughout the lawn area. Your landscaping will appear choppy and abrupt instead of flowing easily with soft curves. Before planting shrubs, have an overall landscaping plan in which you can see how shrub beds relate to the rest of the garden.

Does the shrub create excessive litter? Like trees, shrubs can create litter that you may have to clean up. Check to see if the shrub you choose drops excessive flowers, twigs, pods, or fruit and if the litter is difficult to clean up. Most of the flowering shrubs are not a problem, for fallen blossoms often serve as a mulching component.

Is the shrub compatible with your climate? For your region choose hardy shrubs that do not require extra protection against freezing conditions or hard winds. You don't want to have to bother covering shrubs for winter or staking them against wind.

Minimizing shrub care

After you have selected and planted your shrubs, use a mulch underneath them. This will keep weeds down and retain moisture; you will not have to bother with cultivating around shrubs if you use a mulch.

Consider planting a shade-type ground cover, such as *Pachysandra terminalis* or *Vinca minor*, in shrub beds to absorb droppings from the shrubs and keep down the weeds.

If shrubs are properly spaced, you'll only need to prune them once a year or every two years if necessary. Early in the spring after frost danger has passed, take your annual shrub-pruning garden walk, pruning, shaping, and removing dead wood where necessary. Then leave the shrubs alone until the following year.

(Turn page for Shrubs chart)

Low Shrubs (Under 6 ft.)

NAME	HARDINESS ZONES	EVERGREEN OR DECIDUOUS	SUN OR SHADE	SIZE	COMMENTS
AGAVE attenuata	9-10	E	Sun	To 2½ ft. by 5 ft.	Soft green succulent. Forms a trunk in age. Protect from frost, hot sun.
ARCTOSTAPHYLOS densiflora VINE HILL MANZANITA	8-9*	E	Sun	Low and spreading	Outer branches root. Likes loose soil, good drainage.
A. uva-ursi BEARBERRY, KINNIKINNICK	3-8**	E	Sun	To 15 ft. wide	Leathery leaves turn red in winter; white or pinkish flowers, red or pink fruits. Drought tolerant.
ARTEMESIA abrotanum SOUTHERNWOOD, OLD MAN	4-10	D-E	Sun	To 3-5 ft.	Lemon-scented, green feathery foliage. Yellowish white flowers. Drought resistant.
ASPLENIUM bulbiferum MOTHER FERN	9-10	E	Shade	Fronds to 4 ft. long	Graceful, finely cut fronds. Watch for snails and slugs.
AZALEAS	3-10	D-E	Part shade	Varies	Many types. Southern indicas are vigorous and take sun. Wide range of bloom colors and seasons.
BERBERIS mentorensis BARBERRY	5-9	D-E	Sun	To 7 ft. by 7 ft.	Evergreen to −5°. Compact growth. Makes a good hedge.
B. thunbergii JAPANESE BARBERRY	5-10	D	Sun	To 4-6 ft.	Various fall leaf colors. Red berries through winter. Good hedge.
B. verruculosa WARTY BARBERRY	6-9	E	Sun	To 3-4 ft.	Very neat, compact. Black berries.
BUXUS harlandii DWARF BOXWOOD	8-10	E	Sun-shade	To 3 ft.	One of smallest boxwoods. Easy to neglect but looks better with care.
B. microphylla LITTLELEAF BOXWOOD	5-8	E	Sun-shade	To 3-5 ft.	*B.m. japonica* is taller, takes alkaline soil; *B.m. koreana* grows lower, more slowly.
CALLUNA vulgaris SCOTCH HEATHER	5-8	E	Sun	To 15-30 in.	Many good varieties, flowers from white to crimson.
CAMELLIA sasanqua	7-10	E	Some sun	Varies	Some upright, others bushy or spreading. Profuse bloom.
CEANOTHUS griseus	7-10	E	Sun	To 2-8 ft.	Spreading to upright form. Don't overwater. Dense, violet flower clusters.
CHAMAECYPARIS lawsoniana 'Minima Glauca' LITTLE BLUE CYPRESS	6-9	E	Sun-shade	To 3 ft. by 2½ ft.	Compact, nearly globular form. Blue-green foliage.
CISTUS hybridus WHITE ROCKROSE	8-10	E	Sun	To 2-5 ft. by 2-5 ft.	White spring bloom. Fast growing, drought resistant, tolerates poor soil.
C. salvifolius SAGELEAF ROCKROSE	8-10	E	Sun	To 2 ft. by 6 ft.	Profuse white bloom. Good bank or ground cover for dry, poor soil.
COTONEASTER apiculata CRANBERRY COTONEASTER	5-9	D	Sun	To 4 ft.	Red fruits, pink flowers. 'Blackburn' is compact, has larger fruits.
C. glaucophylla BRIGHT-BEAD COTONEASTER	7-10	E	Sun	To 6 ft. by 6 ft.	Pinkish flowers, dull red fruits. Best in dry, poor soil.
C. horizontalis ROCK COTONEASTER	6-9	D	Sun	To 2-3 ft. by 15 ft.	Out of leaf a short time. White flowers, mass of shiny red fruits. Allow room to spread.
C. microphylla ROCKSPRAY COTONEASTER	7-9	E	Sun	To 2-3 ft. by 6 ft.	Branches root. Thrives with neglect.

*Except in South
**Except Zones 5, 6, 7 in East

NAME	HARDINESS ZONES	EVERGREEN OR DECIDUOUS	SUN OR SHADE	SIZE	COMMENTS
CYTISUS kewensis KEW BROOM	6-8	Semi-E	Sun	To 10 in. by 4 ft.	Branches cascade over wall or bank. White spring flowers.
C. praecox WARMINSTER BROOM, MOONLIGHT BROOM	6-8	Semi-E	Sun	To 3-5 ft. by 4-6 ft.	Informal screen or hedge. Profuse creamy spring flowers.
DAPHNE odora WINTER DAPHNE	8-9	E	Part shade	To 4 ft.	Fragrant bloom, unpredictable behavior. Don't over-water.
ENKIANTHUS campanulatus	5-10*	D	Light shade	To 20 ft.	Handsome, slow growing. Red fall foliage.
ERICA carnea HEATH	6-8	E	Sun-part shade	To 6-16 in.	Varieties in white, red, pink bloom. Prune annually to keep compact.
ESCALLONIA 'Alice'	8-10	E	Sun-shade	To 3-4 ft.	Compact. Glossy leaves. Bright red flowers.
EUONYMUS alatus 'Compactus' DWARF WINGED EUONYMUS	3-10	D	Sun	To 4-6 ft. by 4-6 ft.	Wing-shaped twigs, red fall foliage.
E. fortunei WINTER CREEPER	4-7	E	Sun	Varies by kind	Species 'Colorata' and 'Vegata' have sprawling habit. 'Sarcoxie' more upright.
FORSYTHIA viridissima 'Bronxensis' GREENSTEM FORSYTHIA	5-8	D	Sun	To 16 in.	Slow growing. Heavy flower production. Tolerates most soils.
GARDENIA jasminoides	8-10**	E	Sun-shade	To 1-5 ft.	Prolific, white, fragrant bloom. Needs warmth, ample water.
GAULTHERIA shallon SALAL	6-8**	E	Sun-shade	To 4-10 ft.	Low growth in sun, poor soil. Blooms March-June.
HEBE buxifolia BOXLEAF HEBE	9-10	E	Sun-shade	To 5 ft.	White summer flowers. Rounded, symmetrical shrub. Other hebes have purplish foliage. Needs good drainage. Often called *Veronica*.
HYPERICUM moserianum GOLD FLOWER	7-10	E	Sun-shade	To 3 ft.	Moundlike habit, yellow summer blooms. Takes drought, poor soil.
ILEX crenata JAPANESE HOLLY	7-10	E	Sun-shade	Varies by kind	Small varieties (to 24 in.) look more like boxwood than holly: *I. c.* 'Compacta,' 'Green Island,' 'Green Thumb,' 'Helleri.'
I.c. 'Convexa'	6-9	E	Sun-shade	To 4-6 ft.	Compact, rounded, broader than tall. Convex leaves.
JASMINUM floridum FLORIDA JASMINE	7-10	E, Semi-E	Sun-shade	To 3-4 ft.	Yellow flower clusters in spring-fall. Adjusts to most soils.
JUNIPERUS chinensis 'Armstrongii' ARMSTRONG JUNIPER	4-10	E	Sun	To 4 ft. by 4 ft.	Upright, compact. Needs good drainage.
J.c. 'San Jose'	4-10	E	Sun	To 2 ft. by 6 ft.	Prostrate, dense, slow growing.
J. communis depressa PASTURE JUNIPER, OLDFIELD JUNIPER	3-9	E	Sun	To 4 ft.	Many stems rise from base.
J. conferta SHORE JUNIPER	6-10	E	Sun	To 1 ft. by 6-8 ft.	Prostrate, trailing. Takes heat, needs well-drained soil.

*Except in Midwest
**Except Zones 9, 10 in West

NAME	HARDINESS ZONES	EVERGREEN OR DECIDUOUS	SUN OR SHADE	SIZE	COMMENTS
J. horizontalis PROSTRATA JUNIPER	3-10	E	Sun	To 18 in. by 10 ft.	Flat, heavy branches. *J.h.* 'Wiltonii (Blue carpet juniper) is intense silver blue.
J. sabina SAVIN JUNIPER	5-10	E	Sun	To 4 ft. by 10 ft.	Several good varieties. *J.s.* 'Tamariscifolia' makes good ground cover.
J. squamata SINGLESEED JUNIPER	5-10	E	Sun	To 3 ft.	Compact habit. *J.s.* 'Meyeri' more upright.
LEUCOPHYLLUM frutescens TEXAS RANGER	8-10	E	Sun	To 5-12 ft. by 4-6 ft.	Compact, slow growing. Needs heat to produce rose-purple summer flowers.
LEUCOTHOE davisiae	6-7	E	Part shade	To 3½ ft.	Best in masses, wet places. White summer bloom.
LIGUSTRUM vulgare 'Lodense' COMMON PRIVET	5-10	D	Sun-part shade	To 4 ft. by 4 ft.	Dense growth. Light green foliage.
MAHONIA aquifolium OREGON GRAPE	7-9	E	Sun-shade	To 6 ft.	Looks good all year. Lower growing varieties include *M.a.* 'Compacta,' 'Mahani,' 'Nana.'
M. nervosa LONGLEAF MAHONIA	6-9	E	Shade	To 2 ft.	Spreads by underground stems. Yellow flowers. Needs ample water.
M. repens CREEPING MAHONIA	5-8	E	Sun-part shade	To 3 ft.	Winter leaf color, summer bloom. Spreads by underground stems.
MYRTUS communis 'Compacta' DWARF MYRTLE	8-10	E	Sun-part shade	To 1-2 ft.	Glossy, aromatic leaves. Takes any soil, needs good drainage.
NANDINA domestica 'Nana' HEAVENLY BAMBOO	7-10	E	Sun-part shade	To 12-18 in.	Delicate foliage, good leaf color.
PINUS mugo mughus MUGHO PINE	3-6	E	Sun	To 4 ft.	Slow growing conifer. Shrubby, symmetrical.
POTENTILLA fruticosa BUSH CINQUEFOIL	3-6	D	Sun	To 2-5 ft.	Blooms from June-October; tolerates poor soil, heat, drought.

LEFT: Arctostaphylos densiflora *(Manzanita) is California native.* **Center:** Pittosporum tobira 'Variegata' *(Tobira).* **Right:** *Shade-loving* fatsia japonica *(Japanese aralia) left of* Aucuba japonica *(Japanese aucuba).*

NAME	HARDINESS ZONES	EVERGREEN OR DECIDUOUS	SUN OR SHADE	SIZE	COMMENTS
PYRACANTHA coccinea FIRETHORN	5-10*	E	Sun	To 3 ft.	Glossy leaves, bright berries. Low varieties: *P.c.* 'Peter Pan,' 'Red Elf,' 'Santa Cruz,' 'Tiny Tim.'
RAPHIOLEPIS indica INDIA HAWTHORN	8-10	E	Sun	To 4-5 ft.	Leathery leaves, pinkish bloom. Stays compact. Many good varieties.
RHAPIS excelsa LADY PALM	9-10	E	Part shade	To 5-12 ft.	Grows in clumps. Tolerates drought.
RIBES cereum SQUAW CURRANT	5-8**	D	Sun	To 3 ft.	Bright red fruit, white flowers.
ROSMARINUS officinalis ROSEMARY	8-10	E	Sun	To 2-6 ft.	Dark green, aromatic foliage. Blue flowers. Endures hot sun, poor soil, needs good drainage.
SANTOLINA chamaecyparissus LAVENDER COTTON	7-10	E	Sun	To 2 ft.	Whitish gray leaves, little yellow flowers. Any soil. Looks best if pruned.
SARCOCOCCA humilis	7-10	E	Sun-shade	To 1½ ft.	Glossy foliage hides fragrant, tiny, white spring flowers. Glossy blue-black fruit.
S. ruscifolia	8-10	E	Sun-shade	To 4-6 ft.	Glossy leaves, fragrant flowers, red fruit. Forms natural espalier.
SEVERINIA buxifolia CHINESE BOX-ORANGE	9-10	E	Sun	To 6 ft	Spiny plant good for barriers.
SKIMMIA japonica	7-9	E	Part shade	To 2-5 ft. by 3-6 ft.	Slow growing. Fragrant flowers, red berries.
S. reevesiana	7-9	E	Part shade	To 2 ft.	Glossy leaves, white flower clusters, red fall-winter fruit.
SPIRAEA billiardii	3-8	D	Sun-shade	To 4-6 ft.	Good filler; spreads by underground stems. Pink flowers.
STEPHANANDRA incisa 'Crispa'	6-8	D	Sun	To 1½-3 ft.	Compact habit, fine texture, fall color.
SYMPHORICARPOS chenaultii CHENAULT CORALBERRY	6-8	D	Sun-shade	To 3 ft. by 12 ft.	Spreads like a wild thicket. Good for erosion control.
TAXUS cuspidata 'Nana' JAPANESE YEW	5-8	E	Sun-shade	To 4 ft. by 7 ft.	Slow-growing. More shade and moisture tolerant than most conifers.
T. media 'Brownii' GLOBE YEW	6-9	E	Sun-shade	To 4-8 ft.	Good for low, dense hedge. Slow-growing, compact.
TERNSTROEMIA gymnanthera	8-10	E	Sun-part shade	To 3-4 ft. by 4-6 ft.	Glossy, leathery foliage; reddish new growth. Needs ample moisture.
VACCINIUM ovatum EVERGREEN HUCKLEBERRY	7-8**	E	Part shade	Varies by location	Grows to 2-3 ft. in sun, 8-10 ft. in shade. Bronzy new growth.
VIBURNUM davidii	8-9***	E	Shade	To 1-3 ft. by 3-4 ft.	White flower clusters, turquoise berries.
V. opulus 'Nanum' DWARF EUROPEAN CRANBERRY BUSH	3-9	D	Sun-shade	To 2 ft. by 2 ft.	Needs no trimming as low hedge. Takes poor, wet soils. No flowers, fruit.
YUCCA filamentosa ADAM'S NEEDLE	4-10	E	Sun	To 2½ ft.	White flower spikes rise to 7 ft. above plant. Drought tolerant.
Y. glauca SMALL SOAPWEED	3-10	E	Sun	To 2½ ft.	Stemless or short-stemmed. Greenish white flowers, tall clusters.

*Except Zones 5, 6 in Midwest
**Except in East, Midwest
***Except in West

NAME	HARDINESS ZONES	EVERGREEN OR DECIDUOUS	SUN OR SHADE	SIZE	COMMENTS
ABELIA grandiflora GLOSSY ABELIA	7-10	E	Sun	To 8 ft. by 5 ft.	Graceful habit, bronzy new growth. Summer bloom.
ARBUTUS unedo STRAWBERRY TREE	8-10	E	Sun-shade	To 8-35 ft.	Performs well in extremes of climate and soil. Handsome trunk, colorful fall-winter fruit.
AUCUBA japonica JAPANESE AUCUBA	7-10	E	Shade	To 10 ft.	Many variegated forms. Needs ample water, tolerates many soils.
AZALEAS	3-10	D-E	Part-full shade	To 25 ft.	Deciduous azaleas even more showy than evergreen types.
BAUHINIA galpinii RED BAUHINIA	9-10	E	Sun	To 15 ft.	Sprawling habit. Spectacular red to orange flowers. Best espaliered on warm wall.
BUXUS sempervirens COMMON BOXWOOD, ENGLISH BOXWOOD	6-10	E	Sun-shade	To 15-20 ft.	Dense foliage, billowing growth. Dies in hot summer areas, alkaline soils.
CALLISTEMON citrinus LEMON BOTTLEBRUSH	8-10	E	Sun	To 10-15 ft.	Bright red, brushlike flowers throughout year. Fast growing. Tolerates heat, cold, most soils.
CAMELLIA	7-10	E	Shade	To 6-12 ft.	Requires rich, well-drained soil. *C. japonica* favored; *C. sasanqua* takes sun.
CARAGANA arborescens SIBERIAN PEA-SHRUB	3-9	D	Sun	To 20 ft.	Yellow spring flowers resemble sweet peas. Fast growing. Good in climate extremes, drought, poor soil.
CARISSA grandiflora NATAL PLUM	9-10	E	Sun	To 5-7 ft.	White, fragrant flowers; red fruit. Adapts to many soils, exposures.
CASSIA artemisioides FEATHERY CASSIA	9-10	E	Sun	To 6-8 ft.	Airy, delicate. Yellow flowers January-April.
CEANOTHUS impressus SANTA BARBARA CEANOTHUS	8-10	E	Sun	To 4-10 ft.	Fast growing, wide spreading. Deep blue flowers.
C. 'Julia Phelps'	8-10	E	Sun	To 6-8 ft. by 8-10 ft.	Stunning as big screen or single shrub.
CLEYERA japonica	8-10	E	Part shade	To 6-8 ft. by 6-8 ft.	Graceful, arching branches. Dark red new growth. Slow growing.
COPROSMA repens MIRROR PLANT	8-10	E	Part shade	To 10 ft. by 6 ft.	Shiny leaves. Needs pruning twice a year to keep dense.
CORNUS alba 'Sibirica' SIBERIAN DOGWOOD	3-9	D	Sun	To 7 ft. by 5 ft.	Bright red bark all winter. Yellowish-white flowers.
C. racemosa GRAY DOGWOOD	5-8	D	Sun	To 15 ft.	Dense growth, purple fall foliage, profuse summer bloom.
C. stolonifera REDTWIG DOGWOOD, REDOSIER DOGWOOD	4-8	D	Sun	To 15 ft.	Brilliant fall color, red winter twigs. Thrives in poor soil.
CORTADERIA selloana PAMPAS GRASS	6-10	E	Sun	To 20 ft.	Fast growing giant ornamental grass with feathery plumes. Tolerates any soil.
COTONEASTER divaricata SPREADING COTONEASTER	5-9	D	Sun	To 6-7 ft.	Profuse pink flowers, showy fruits.

NAME	HARDINESS ZONES	EVERGREEN OR DECIDUOUS	SUN OR SHADE	SIZE	COMMENTS
C. lactea	6-10	E	Sun	To 6-8 ft.	Arching growth. Red, long-lasting fruits.
C. pannosa SILVERLEAF COTONEASTER	7-10	E	Sun	To 10 ft.	Arching branches. Good wind screen.
CYCAS revoluta SAGO PALM	8-10	E	Part shade	To 10 ft.	Long, featherlike leaves. Slow growing.
DODONAEA viscosa HOPBUSH, HOPSEED	8-10	E	Sun	To 12-15 ft.	Fast growing; wide spreading. 'Purpurea' has bronzy leaves. Tolerates poor soil, drought, desert heat.
EUONYMUS alatus WINGED EUONYMUS	3-10	D	Sun	To 7-10 ft.	Dark green leaves turn red in fall. Horizontal branching.
E. japonica EVERGREEN EUONYMUS	7-9	E	Sun	To 8-10 ft.	Glossy, leathery leaves. High tolerance for heat, poor soil.
E. kiautschovica	6-8	E	Sun	To 9 ft.	Showy fruits, E.k. 'Du Pont' Is compact, fast growing.
FALLUGIA paradoxa APACHE PLUME	5-10*	Semi-E	Sun	To 3-8 ft.	Flowers like single white roses. Fruit clusters follow.
FATSIA japonica JAPANESE ARALIA	8-10	E	Shade	To 5-8 ft.	Big, glossy, tropical leaves. Dramatic in shaded entryway. Takes some sun, nearly all soils.
FEIJOA sellowiana PINEAPPLE GUAVA	8-10	E	Sun	To 18-25 ft.	Subtropical fruits. Trains to any shape.
FONTANESIA fortunei	0-7	D	Sun	To 15 ft.	Graceful foliage. Small greenish-white flowers.
FORSYTHIA 'Beatrix Farrand'	5-8	D	Sun	To 7-10 ft.	Fountain-shaped shrub with dependable, profuse bloom.
F. intermedia BORDER FORSYTHIA	5-9	D	Sun	To 10 ft.	F.i. 'Karl Sax' neat, graceful. F.i. 'Lynwood' grows stiff, upright.
F. viridissima GREENSTEM FORSYTHIA	5-8	D	Sun	To 10 ft.	Stiff-looking. F.v. 'Bronxensis' 16 in. dwarf, slow growing.
HAMAMELIS WITCH HAZEL	5-8	D	Sun-light shade	To 10 ft.	Fragrant, yellow flowers, yellow fall foliage.
HETEROMELES arbutifolia TOYON, CALIFORNIA HOLLY, CHRISTMAS BERRY					See Small Trees.
HYDRANGEA arborescens 'Grandiflora' HILLS OF SNOW	4-9	D	Part shade	To 10 ft.	Dense, upright growth. Large flower clusters, sterile flowers.
ILEX altaclarensis 'Wilsonii' WILSON HOLLY	7-10	E	Sun-shade	To 6-8 ft.	One of best hollies. Takes almost any soil, sun, shade, wind.
I. cornuta 'Burfordii' BURFORD HOLLY	7-10	E	Sun	To 10 ft.	Spineless leaves. Needs long, warm season to set fruit.
I. crenata JAPANESE HOLLY	6-10	E	Sun	To 20 ft.	Compact, rounded shrub. Looks like boxwood. Berries are black.
I. glabra INKBERRY	3-9	E	Sun	To 9-20 ft.	I.g. 'Compacta' lower, more dense. Tolerates swampy areas.
I. vomitoria YAUPON	8-10	E	Sun	To 15-20 ft.	Stands extreme alkaline soils, narrow, dark green leaves.

*Except in East, Midwest

NAME	HARDINESS ZONES	EVERGREEN OR DECIDUOUS	SUN OR SHADE	SIZE	COMMENTS
IXORA coccinea FLAME-OF-THE-WOODS	9-10*	E	Sun	To 15 ft.	Brilliant yellow, red flowers bloom most of year.
JUNIPERUS chinensis 'Pfitzeriana' PFITZER JUNIPER	4-10	E	Sun	To 5-6 ft. by 15-20 ft.	Arching, gray-green conifer. Sharp-needled foliage.
J. communis 'Stricta'	4-10	E	Sun	To 12-20 ft.	Narrow column with compact branch tips. Dark green foliage.
J. c. 'Torulosa' HOLLYWOOD JUNIPER	4-10	E	Sun	To 15 ft.	Irregular, twisted appearance. Needs room.
KOLKWITZIA amabilis BEAUTY BUSH	5-9	D	Sun-shade	To 10-12 ft.	Heavy spring-summer bloom. Upright in part shade, dense, lower in full sun.
LAGERSTROEMIA indica CRAPE MYRTLE	8-10	D	Sun	To 6-30 ft.	Long flowering season. Slow growing. Needs deep watering.
LEPTOSPERMUM laevigatum 'Reevesii' AUSTRALIAN TEA TREE	9-10	E	Sun	To 6-7 ft.	Picturesque, twisted trunk. Thick screen as hedge, needs well-drained, slightly acid soil.
LIGUSTRUM japonicum JAPANESE PRIVET, WAXLEAF PRIVET	7-10	E	Sun-shade	To 10-12 ft.	Dense, compact growth good for hedges or screens.
L. obtusifolium BORDER PRIVET	5-9	E	Sun	To 9 ft.	Horizontal branches make beautiful unclipped hedge. Hardiest of privets.
KALMIA latifolia MOUNTAIN LAUREL	5-8*	E	Part shade	To 6-8 ft. by 6-8 ft.	Pink spring flowers give ample blossom effect. Slow growing.
MISCANTHUS sinensis EULALIA GRASS	5-10	E	Sun	To 10 ft.	Ornamental, gracefully arching stalks. Feathery, foot-long fruit stalks.
MYRICA pensylvanica BAYBERRY	3-8	D-E	Sun	To 9 ft.	Compact growth; takes poor, sandy soil.
NANDINA domestica HEAVENLY BAMBOO	7-10	E	Sun-part shade	To 6-8 ft.	Light, airy, colorful effect. Year-round leaf color, bright red berries.
NERIUM oleander OLEANDER	8-10	E	Sun	To 12 ft.	Wide shrub. Long bloom season. Takes poor soil, drought, heat.
OSMANTHUS delavayi DELAVAY OSMANTHUS	7-9	E	Sun-part shade	To 4-6 ft.	Large, white, fragrant flowers. Slow growing; graceful branches.
O. fortunei 'San Jose'	8-10	E	Sun-part shade	To 6-20 ft.	Hollylike leaves. Cream, orange flowers in fall.
PHOTINIA fraseri	8-10	E	Sun	To 10 ft.	New growth bronzy red, showy. Resists mildew; good espalier.
P. glabra JAPANESE PHOTINIA	8-9	E	Sun	To 6-10 ft.	Broad, dense growth, coppery when new. Needs summer pruning.
PIERIS floribunda MOUNTAIN PIERIS	6-7	E	Part shade	To 3-6 ft.	Looks good year-round. Needs same care as rhododendrons, azaleas.
P. japonica LILY-OF-THE-VALLEY SHRUB	7-9	E	Part shade	To 9-10 ft.	Reddish new growth, drooping flower clusters.
PITTOSPORUM tenuifolium	9-10	E	Sun-part shade	To 40 ft.	Dense, hedge plant. Wavy, glossy, deep green foliage.

*Except in West

NAME	HARDINESS ZONES	EVERGREEN OR DECIDUOUS	SUN OR SHADE	SIZE	COMMENTS
P. tobira TOBIRA	9-10	E	Sun-shade	To 6-15 ft.	'Variegata' smaller, white-edged foliage. Shiny leaves, white flower clusters.
P. undulatum VICTORIAN FOX	9-10	E	Sun-part shade	To 30-40 ft.	Prune for a lower, dense screen. Don't plant near lawn or paving where fruits can be messy.
PODOCARPUS macrophyllus YEW PINE	8-10	E	Sun-shade	To 50 ft.	Narrow, upright, easily pruned to shape.
PRUNUS besseyi WESTERN SAND CHERRY	5-8	D	Sun	To 7 ft.	White blossoms, black fruits.
P. caroliniana CAROLINA LAUREL CHERRY	8-10	E	Sun	To 20-30 ft.	Dense foliage, some litter. Black fruit, small spring flowers.
PSIDIUM cattleianum STRAWBERRY GUAVA	8-10	E	Sun	To 8-10 ft.	Beautiful bark and trunk. Glossy leaves, dark red fruit.
PYRACANTHA coccinea FIRETHORN	5-10	E	Sun	To 10-20 ft.	Many shapes, sizes. 'Lalandei' hardiest.
RAPHIOLEPIS umbellata	8-10	E	Sun	To 10 ft.	Roundish, leathery leaves. Vigorous, thick, and bushy.
RHAMNUS alaternus ITALIAN BUCKTHORN	8-10	E	Sun-part shade	To 12-20 ft.	Fast, dense growth; wide spreading. Takes drought, heat, wind.
R. frangula 'Columnaris' TALLHEDGE BUCKTHORN	3-8	D	Sun	To 12-15 ft. by 4 ft.	Good hedge for cold-winter areas. Needs minimum trimming.
RHODODENDRON	5-9	E-D	Shade	To 6 ft.	Many types, flower colors. All need acid soil, continual moisture.
RHUS typhina STAGHORN SUMAC	3-9	D	Sun	To 15-30 ft.	See *Small Trees.*
ROBINIA neo mexicana NEW MEXICAN LOCUST	6-10	E	Sun	To 6 ft.	Rose-like flowers in June-August.
SOPHORA secundiflora MESCAL BEAN, TEXAS MOUNTAIN LAUREL	8-10	E	Sun	To 25 ft.	Slow growth. Can be trained as a tree. Spring blooms in clusters.
SYRINGA vulgaris COMMON LILAC	3-8	D	Sun	To 20 ft.	Plants must go dormant to bloom well. Hundreds of varieties.
TAXUS baccata 'Stricta' IRISH YEW	6-7	E	Sun-part shade	To 20 ft.	Dark green foliage. Slow growing. Drought tolerant once established.
THRYALLIS glauca RAIN-OF-GOLD	10*		Sun	To 9 ft.	Yellow flower clusters.
VACCINIUM corymbosum HIGHBUSH BLUEBERRY	5-7	D	Sun	To 6-12 ft.	Vigorous growth, brilliant autumn color, heavy fruit production. Needs acid soil.
VIBURNUM	See comments	D-E	Sun-shade	Varies by kind	Some grown for foliage, some for flowers. *V. dentatum, V. lantana* zones 3-8.
V. plicatum tomentosum DOUBLEFILE VIBURNUM	5-10	D	Sun-shade	To 2 ft. by 2 ft.	Flat flower clusters; fruit. Red, showy.
XYLOSMA congestum	8-10	D-E	Sun-part shade	To 8-10 ft.	Loose, graceful shrub tolerates heat, most soils.
YUCCA recurvifolia	8-10	E	Sun	To 6-10 ft.	Single trunk or lightly branched. Spreads to make large groups.

Except in West

Ground Covers...
step up from slavery

Compact and versatile in color and texture, ground covers are living carpets that solve many maintenance problems. Probably the widest use of ground cover in a low maintenance garden occurs when it is planted as a lawn substitute. Almost every garden has trouble spots where lawn is difficult to grow. One of the most difficult spots is in heavy shade and under large trees where soil is poor and roots abound. Such hardy ground covers as the English or Algerian ivies or *Pachysandra terminalis* will alleviate coping with a sickly lawn in these areas, provide esthetic appeal, and swallow up material dropped from trees.

Another primary use of ground cover as a maintenance aid occurs when it is planted on a rocky hillside or a steep slope, where it helps with erosion problems and eliminates the necessity for mowing. In some climates, ice plant is an excellent ground cover for sloping areas, as many freeway plantings of this colorful succulent testify.

Probably the biggest drawback to using a ground cover is that it will take a fair amount of time to get established, usually about two years. In the initial phases, you will have to do more watering, weeding, and fertilizing. But once a ground cover is established, you'll have to do little else but trim it occasionally and water now and then when needed. A hardy, established ground cover will hold its own against adversity.

One solution to the disadvantage of a ground cover taking longer to get established is to plant annuals in between until the ground cover fills in. In addition to adding color, this eliminates some of the problems with weeding. For example, if you are planting some English ivy underneath a large shade tree, you could plant some primroses in between the ivy clusters or put in summer impatiens.

Questions to ask about a ground cover

As with all low maintenance plants, you must ask very specific questions before choosing the right ground cover for the right site:

Is the plant invasive? Some ground covers are such good growers that they can become pests by spreading out into other areas and smothering other plant growth. Hall's Japanese honeysuckle (*Lonicera japonica* 'Halliana') is one of these invasive ground covers. It is fast growing and covers ground very well, especially on slopes. But it is so vigorous that it must be controlled with sharp shears or it will become a nuisance.

Varieties of polygonum are very good ground covers in exceptionally tough spots where very little will grow, but this plant can also become a pest in the improper area. You should think about the site where you want the ground cover to be placed. If it is in a fairly formal or tight area, such as an entryway, you don't want an aggressive ground cover. But if you want to plant a fast grower in a more casual area of the garden, you may not care how fast it grows. Ajuga, which is a very hardy and versatile ground cover, may spread out into the lawn, but it can be mowed along with the grass with no harm to the ajuga.

Does the ground cover require a lot of pruning to grow well? Some ground covers may get scraggly or stringy looking if they are not cut back. Creeping St. Johnswort (*Hypericum calycinum*) is a tough, dense ground cover for sun or shade, but in order to look its best, the tops should be clipped or mowed off every two years. You may want to choose instead a ground cover such as ajuga that also thrives in sun or shade and will grow to its natural height, looking compact and healthy without having to be cut back.

Does the ground cover need sun or shade to grow well? It will not do in a low maintenance garden to try to grow a sun-loving ground cover, such as gazania, in the shade, or a shade lover, such as Japanese spurge (*Pachysandra terminalis*) in hot sun. You'll have a constant struggle keeping them alive. Check your garden sources about the specific nature of the ground cover. Many ground covers —such as English or Algerian ivy and ajuga—grow equally well in sun or shade.

Does the ground cover grow successfully in a variety of soil and moisture conditions? Among the most popular ground covers throughout the United States that will grow under many conditions and resist most pests and diseases are English ivy, *Pachysandra terminalis*, and *Vinca minor*. Ajuga is also very popular, although it takes a lot of water. These ground covers form a good, solid cover, propagate easily, and tolerate a mild amount of traffic. Your climate, of course, will determine ground covers for your specific use, so check the chart in this chapter for more details. Sunset's *Lawn and Ground Cover* book offers further suggestions of ground covers for your area.

Minimizing ground cover care

If you are concerned with keeping a ground cover area clean and free from litter, think about another method besides raking—a difficult approach at best. A hose is effective in squirting out loose materials, or you can use a broom to sweep over the top of the ground cover.

If you plant a ground cover next to grass and you don't want the ground cover to spread, use a brick or redwood mowing strip so that the ground cover doesn't grow into the grass. If your garden is more natural appearing, let the ground cover grow where it chooses.

NAME	HARDINESS ZONES	SUN OR SHADE	APPROX. HEIGHT	COMMENTS
AJUGA reptans CARPET BUGLE	4-10	Sun-shade	10 in.	Dark green mat with blue flower spikes. Needs regular watering, good drainage.
ARCTOSTAPHYLOS uva-ursi KINNIKINNICK, BEARBERRY				See *Low Shrubs.*
ARCTOTHECA calendula CAPE WEED	8-10	Sun	12 in.	Abundant yellow daisies in spring.
ASPARAGUS densiflorus 'Sprengeri' SPRENGER ASPARAGUS	9-10	Sun-shade	3 ft.	Needlelike leaves, billowy effect, red berries. Needs temperatures above 24°.
BACCHARIS pilularis DWARF COYOTE BRUSH, DWARF CHAPARRAL BROOM	9-10	Sun	8-24 in.	Dense mat spreads to 6 ft. or more. Almost any climate or soil.
CAMPANULA poscharskyana SERBIAN BELLFLOWER	4-10	Sun-shade	12 in.	Vigorous; stands some drought. Lavender spring bloom.
CARPOBROTUS edulis ICE PLANT	9-10*	Sun	6 in.	Fast-growing succulent. Tolerates most soils, drought. Pale yellow to rose flowers.
CEANOTHUS gloriosus POINT REYES CEANOTHUS				See *Low Shrubs.*
C. prostratus SQUAW CARPET, MAHALA MAT	5-8*	Sun	2 in.	Dense mat, spreads to 8 ft. wide. Especially good at higher elevations.
CERASTIUM tomentosum SNOW-IN-SUMMER	4-10**	Sun	6-8 in.	Grayish, woolly foliage. Spreads quickly. Takes neglect.
CHLOROPHYTUM comosum SPIDER PLANT	9-10	Part shade	1-3 ft.	Clumps form from main plant and take root.
CORONILLA varia CROWN VETCH	4-10	Part shade	2 ft.	A tenacious legume, difficult to eliminate when established. Dormant in winter.
COTONEASTER dammeri BEARBERRY COTONEASTER	6-10	Sun-part shade	3-6 in.	Spreads to 10 ft.; branches root. Showy white flowers, red fruit.
EUONYMUS fortunei 'Colorata' PURPLE-LEAF WINTER CREEPER	5-9	Sun-shade	6 in.	Spreads to 20 ft. Leaves turn purple in fall and winter.
FRAGARIA chiloensis WILD STRAWBERRY, SAND STRAWBERRY	7-10	Sun-shade	6-12 in.	Forms compact, lush mats; bright red fruit in fall. Needs regular watering.
GAZANIA	9-10	Sun	6-10 in.	Bright, daisy flowers bloom intermittently throughout year in mild areas. Both clumping and trailing types.
HEDERA canariensis ALGERIAN IVY	8-10	Sun-shade	12 in.	Bright green, wide leaves suited to large areas. More tolerant of hot sun than English ivy, requires more water.
H. helix 'Baltica' ENGLISH IVY	5-10	Sun-shade	6 in.	Hardiest variety. Pest free, drought resistant. 'Hahn's self-branching' has smaller leaves.
HEMEROCALLIS DAYLILY	3-10	Sun-shade	1-6 ft.	Tuberous-rooted perennial adapts as ground cover. Stems of lilylike flowers stand well above foliage.
HYPERICUM calycinum AARON'S BEARD, CREEPING ST. JOHNSWORT	6-10	Sun-shade	1 ft.	Bright yellow summer blooms. Tough, dense foliage. Competes successfully with tree roots; takes poor soil, some drought.
JUNIPERUS chinensis sargentii SARGENT JUNIPER, SHIMPAKU	3-10	Sun	1 ft.	Spreads to 10 ft. Feathery, gray-green foliage.

Except in East
Except in Midwest

LEFT: Sagina subulata *(Scotch moss)*, Thymus lanuginosus *(Woolly thyme) cover steps.* **Center:** Polygonum capitatum *(Knotweed) in bloom.* **Right:** *Bright pink* carpobrotus edulis *(Ice plant).*

. . . Ground Covers (continued)

NAME	HARDINESS ZONES	SUN OR SHADE	APPROX. HEIGHT	COMMENTS
LIRIOPE muscari BIG BLUE LILY TURF	7-10	Sun-shade	12-18 in.	Grasslike clumps do not spread. Thrives with lots of moisture. Lilylike flowers.
L. spicata CREEPING LILY TURF	5-10	Sun-shade	8-9 in.	Spreads widely by underground stems. Pale lilac to white flowers. Withstands cold.
LONICERA japonica 'Halliana' HALL'S JAPANESE HONEYSUCKLE	5-10	Sun-shade	8-9 in.	Rampant vine, partly or completely deciduous in coldest regions. Fairly drought resistant; tolerates poor drainage.
LYSIMACHIA nummularia MONEYWORT, CREEPING JENNIE	4-10	Shade	3-6 in.	Light green mat of roundish leaves. Good in low, damp places. Runners root at joints. Summer blooming.
OPHIOPOGON japonicus MONDO GRASS	7-10	Sun-shade	8-12 in.	Billowy carpet of dark green grasslike leaves. Short spikes of lilac flowers in summer.
OSTEOSPERMUM fruticosum TRAILING AFRICAN DAISY	8-10	Sun	6-12 in.	Profusion of daisylike blooms over a long season. Tolerates drought when established.
PACHISTIMA canbyi RATSTRIPPER	4-8	Sun-shade	9-12 in.	Narrow, shiny leaves form compact mat. Needs ample water in hot climates.
PACHYSANDRA terminalis JAPANESE SPURGE	4-9	Shade	6-10 in.	Spreads by underground runners but not aggressive. Fragrant, white flowers in summer; white fruits follow.
PHLOX subulata MOSS PINK	4-9	Sun-shade	6 in.	Sheets of brilliant color in late spring, early summer. Thrives in loose, not too rich soil.
PHYLA nodiflora LIPPIA	9-10	Sun	1 in.	Sturdy enough for lawn.
POLYGONUM capitatum KNOTWEED	8-10	Sun-shade	6 in.	New leaves green, old leaves tinged pink. Invasive roots. Small, pink flowers.
P. cuspidatum compactum JAPANESE KNOTWEED	8-10	Sun	To 24 in.	Red fall leaf color. Showy, reddish flowers. Dies back in winter.
POLYSTICHUM acrostichoides CHRISTMAS FERN	3-10	Part shade	3 ft.	For moist, wooded areas.
POTENTILLA verna SPRING CINQUEFOIL	4-8	Sun-shade	2-6 in.	Dainty, bright green tufted creeper. Use to cover spent bulbs. Takes much moisture.

NAME	HARDINESS ZONES	SUN OR SHADE	APPROX. HEIGHT	COMMENTS
RHOICISSUS capensis EVERGREEN GRAPE	9-10	Sun	1 ft.	Rugged vine good for erosion control on banks. Roots need shade, moisture.
SAGINA subulata IRISH MOSS, SCOTCH MOSS	7-10	Sun-shade	1 in.	Irish moss is rich green; Scotch moss is golden green. Best in limited areas.
SANTOLINA chamaecyparissus LAVENDER COTTON				See *Low Shrubs.*
SEDUM hybridum	7-8	Sun	6 in.	Tiny yellow flowers appear from green mat in spring and late fall.
S. spurium	7-10	Sun	4-5 in.	Rapidly spreading succulent. Drought and heat tolerant. Pink summer flowers.
SYMPHORICARPOS chenaultii CHENAULT CORALBERRY				See *Low Shrubs.*
THYMUS lanuginosus WOOLLY THYME	5-10	Sun	2-3 in.	Forms undulating mat. Use in small areas, between stepping stones, rocks.
T. serpyllum CREEPING THYME	5-10	Sun	2-6 in.	Takes light foot traffic. Soft and fragrant foliage.
TRACHELOSPERMUM jasminoides STAR JASMINE	8-10	Sun-shade	1½-2 ft.	Small, fragrant white flowers on glossy green foliage. Pinch tips for ground cover, otherwise a vine. Blooms June-July.
VACCINIUM angustifolium LOWBUSH BLUEBERRY	5-7*	Sun-part shade	8 in.	Grows wild in northeastern U.S. Tolerates acid soils.
VERONICA incana WOOLLY SPEEDWELL	3-10	Sun	2 ft.	Grayish leaves, blue flower spikes in summer.
VINCA major PERIWINKLE, MYRTLE	7-10	Sun-shade	1-2 ft.	Very invasive; stems root as they spread. *V. minor* is smaller version; less invasive, requires more care.
WALDSTEINIA fragarioides BARREN-STRAWBERRY	5-10	Sun	4 in.	Inedible relative of the strawberry. Adapts to poor, dry soils.
WEDELIA trilobata	9-10	Sun-shade	6 in.	Small yellow flowers.

Except Midwest

Vines...
let them hide the undesirable

Planting a vine in a low maintenance garden is a fast and easy way to cover such eyesores as chain link fences, unsightly wires, poles, rain spouts, tree stumps, or any other objects you would like to have hidden by foliage. Vines will soften and disguise these objects, and because so many vines are flowering, they will add color to your garden. Fast-growing vines also give ready privacy to a yard.

In addition to concealing objectionable objects, vines are also used widely because of their delicacy and esthetic appeal. They add grace to a garden—an old-fashioned appeal reminiscent of what your grandmother may have planted. And they give a nice vertical lift to your garden when all your other plants may have a lower, horizontal look.

Questions to ask about vines

Consider the following questions carefully if you are thinking of planting a vine in your garden:

How rampant is the vine? Some vines grow so rapidly that they can become real problems. The red trumpet vine (*Phaedranthus buccinatorius*, often sold as *Bignonia cherere*) is a rampant grower. It has lovely, trumpet flowers that bloom all summer, but you must make the decision about whether you want the flowers seriously enough to cope with trimming and pruning them or whether you would like to try something less rampant, such as jasmine (*Jasminum officinale*.)

Is the vine long-lived? Many lovely annual vines exist, including sweet pea, morning glory, and nasturtium, but these you have to replant every year. For a low maintenance garden, choose a vine such as the silver lace vine (*Polygonum aubertii*) that will be permanent.

Is the vine hardy for your area? Don't try to grow warm-weather vines in cold climates. A bougainvillea has a tough time in any climate that dips below freezing. One of the most important aspects of low maintenance gardening is choosing plants that are compatible with your climate.

Does the vine drop objectionable litter? Before you buy the vine, check to see if it drops excessive amounts of flowers, fruit, pods, or any other objects that you may have to clean up. Although this is not a common problem with vines, check this factor before you buy.

Does the vine require a lot of work in training? Select a vine that will climb and twine naturally so you do not have to tie it with string or wire to support it. Boston ivy will climb without help on almost any surface. The twining or tendril-type vines will need some support.

Do clinging tendrils damage painted surfaces? Don't grow ivy or any vine with clinging tendrils against the painted surface of a house or fence. If you ever plan to remove the vine, the paint will come off with it; it is almost impossible to remove the fibrous attachments left by the vine.

Will the vine grow into cracks and under shingles? Many vines will grow into any available space. In this case, you should study what the vine's possible growth potential will be. Don't plant a vine where it is able to grow underneath the shingles, through doors, or into spaces in the wall.

Can you remove the vine easily if you have to paint or repair underneath it? Again, consider where you are going to place a vine so you don't have trouble if you have to remove it for painting. Many vines—among them bougainvillea—grow on supports and can very easily be pulled away from the structure while you repair or paint and then placed back again without damaging the vine.

NAME	HARDINESS ZONES	EVERGREEN OR DECIDUOUS	SUN OR SHADE	GROWTH RATE, HEIGHT	COMMENTS
AKEBIA quinata FIVELEAF AKEBIA	5-9	D-E	Sun—shade	Fast to 20 ft.	Dainty leaflets, purple flowers. Slower growing, deciduous in cold winters.
AMPELOPSIS brevipedunculata BLUEBERRY CLIMBER	5-10	D	Sun—shade	Fast to 20 ft.	Lacy vine with turquoise berries. Needs strong support.
ANTIGONON leptopus CORAL VINE, QUEEN'S WREATH, ROSA DE MONTANA	9-10	D-E	Sun	Fast to 40 ft.	Revels in high summer heat. Small pink flowers.
BOUGAINVILLEA	9-10	E	Sun	Varies by kind	Spectacular colors. Don't disturb root ball when planting.
CAMPSIS radicans COMMON TRUMPET CREEPER	5-9	D	Sun	Fast to 40 ft.	Showy, trumpet-shaped flowers. Clings to wood and brick.
CELASTRUS scandens AMERICAN BITTERSWEET	3-8	D	Sun	Fast to 10-20 ft.	Clusters of handsome fruits. Needs support. Best in cold winters.
CISSUS antarctica KANGAROO TREEBINE	9-10	E	Sun—shade	Mod. to 10 ft.	Graceful vine with shiny leaves. Not fussy about soil, water.
C. rhombifolia GRAPE IVY	9-10	E	Sun—shade	Mod. to 20 ft.	Variety 'Mandaiana' is more upright, compact.

LEFT: *White flower clusters on Wisteria venusta (silky wisteria).* **Center:** *Clematis lawsoniana 'Henryi' (Henry clematis) climbs post.* **Right:** *Bougainvillea returns care at planting time with long, splashy bloom.*

NAME	HARDINESS ZONES	EVERGREEN OR DECIDUOUS	SUN OR SHADE	SIZE	COMMENTS
CLEMATIS	4-9	D-E	Sun	Varies by kind	Most species deciduous; grow evergreen *C. armandii* in zones 6-9. Showy flowers on all; need rich, fast-draining soil, mulch to cool roots, plenty of water, fertilizer in growing season.
CLYTOSTOMA callistegioides VIOLET TRUMPET VINE	9-10	E	Sun—shade	Fast to 30 ft.	Lavender flowers. Strong growth needs pruning to control.
DOXANTHA unguis-cati CAT'S CLAW, YELLOW TRUMPET VINE	8-10	Semi-D	Sun	Fast to 25-40 ft.	Grows best in summer heat. Loses all leaves in cold winters.
EUONYMUS fortunei 'Colorata' PURPLE-LEAF WINTER CREEPER					See *Ground Covers.*
FICUS pumila CREEPING FIG	9-10	E	Shade	See comments	Can be slow starting but will cover a building at maturity. Attaches readily. Invasive roots. Delicate, heart-shaped leaves.
GELSEMIUM sempervirens CAROLINA JESSAMINE	8-10	E	Shade	Mod. to 20 ft.	Fragrant, yellow, late winter blooms. Needs ample water. All parts poisonous.
HEDERA helix ENGLISH IVY	6-9	D	Part shade	Varies by kind	Many small-leafed forms. Also see *Ground Covers.*
HYDRANGEA anomala petiolaris CLIMBING HYDRANGEA	5-8	D	Part shade	Mod. to 75 ft.	White flower clusters, bold foliage.
LONICERA hildebrandiana GIANT BURMESE HONEYSUCKLE	9-10	E	Sun	Fast to 80 ft.	Large leaves, fragrant flowers. Needs plenty of water.

NAME	HARDINESS ZONES	EVERGREEN OR DECIDUOUS	SUN OR SHADE	GROWTH RATE, HEIGHT	COMMENTS
L. japonica 'Halliana' HALL'S JAPANESE HONEYSUCKLE					See *Ground Covers*.
L. sempervirens TRUMPET HONEYSUCKLE	4-9	E	Sun— part shade	Mod. to 50 ft.	Showy flowers, scarlet fruit. Shrubby if not supported.
PANDOREA jasminoides BOWER VINE	9-10	E	Sun— part shade	Fast to 20-30 ft.	Glossy foliage. Summer flowers last through fall. Needs ample water.
PARTHENOCISSUS quinquefolia VIRGINIA CREEPER	3-10	D	Sun— shade	Fast to 30 ft.	Orange to scarlet fall color. Clings to walls.
PASSIFLORA alato-caerulea PASSION VINE	8-10	E	Sun	Fast to 20-30 ft.	Blooms all summer. Protect in cold areas.
PHAEDRANTHUS buccinatorius BLOOD-RED TRUMPET VINE	9-10	E	Sun	Fast to 50 ft.	Brilliant flowers appear when weather warms.
PHASEOLUS caracalla SNAIL VINE	9-10	E-D	Sun	Fast to 10-20 ft.	Cream and purple spring-summer blooms. Needs plenty of heat. Comes back after frost.
POLYGONUM aubertii SILVER LACE VINE	5-10	E-D	Sun	Fast to 20 ft.	White flowers in late spring, fall.
PYROSTEGIA venusta FLAME VINE	9-10	E	Sun	Fast to 20 ft.	Large clusters of orange blooms in fall, winter. Thrives in heat, any soil.
ROSA banksiae LADY BANKS' ROSE	7-10	E-D	Sun	Fast to 20 ft.	Yellow or white flowers. Almost immune to disease, aphids.
R. bracteata 'Mermaid' MERMAID ROSE	7-10	E	Part shade	Fast to 30 ft.	Creamy yellow flowers summer, fall, and intermittently throughout mild winters.
TECOMARIA capensis CAPE HONEYSUCKLE	9-10	E	Sun	Fast to 15-25 ft.	Brilliant orange flowers fall, winter. Takes heat, some drought. Needs good drainage.
THUNBERGIA grandiflora SKY FLOWER	9-10	E	Sun	Fast to 20 ft.	Tubular, blue flowers from fall-spring. Comes back after freeze.
TRACHELOSPERMUM jasminoides STAR JASMINE					See *Ground Covers*.
WISTERIA	5-10	D	Sun	Varies by kind	Showy, drooping, violet flowers good in arbor. Any soil, but needs good drainage, ample water. *W. floribunda* best in full sun, more common in East. *W. sinensis* takes shade, more common in West. Training, support essential.

Perennials...
a longer lease on life

In contrast to the annual, which completes its life cycle in one growing season, the perennial will survive for three years or more. In general, the top growth of the perennial dies down each winter and regrows the following spring. Some perennials, such as the acanthus, need to be cut back drastically in order to grow and bloom successfully the next year. Others, such as the helleborus, remain green all year and produce flowers during one particular season. Either way, their advantages outweigh those of annuals for the low maintenance garden.

Questions to ask about perennials

Perennials are often less costly in the long run than annuals, and they often provide "surprise discoveries" each year, sending up blooms you may have forgotten about. But ask yourself these questions to identify perennials that have lower maintenance characteristics:

Does the perennial require staking? Some perennials, such as delphinium, hollyhock, columbine, and some varieties of chrysanthemums, may need staking, depending on how tall they grow in your area. Unless you have a special sentimental attachment to growing a perennial that will need staking, avoid planting these in your low maintenance garden.

Does the perennial require frequent dividing? Some perennials require frequent dividing in order to perform well in the garden, but if planted in a good soil in a fairly deep hole so that roots have plenty of room to expand, most perennials bloom satisfactorily without dividing for 10 years or more. Many perennials, such as the anemone, daylily, helleborus, peony, red hot poker, and oxalis, prefer to be left alone after planting. A few, such as delphinium and lupine, produce their best flowers on young plants, so they should be removed after three years.

Is the perennial long-lived? Some perennials—cyclamen, marguerites, delphinium, and lupine are examples—would be considered short-lived because they have to be replaced every two or three years. Pyrethrum and stokesia are also considered short-lived perennials. Again, you will have to check the nature of perennial growth in your particular climate, but try to choose plants that will perform the longest in your garden with minimum maintenance. In colder climates, peonies can be left for decades, blooming each spring with gorgeous clumps of gaily colored flowers.

Is the perennial compatible with the site you have chosen? In general, the majority of perennials need exposure to the sun and a free circulation of air in order to perform best. A few perennials, such as ferns, daylilies, primroses and helleborus, will do well in partial shade.

Is the perennial suitable to your climate? You'll want to choose the perennials that thrive in your climate. Peonies,

some varieties of bearded iris, and delphinium may not survive in very warm climates because of the heat.

Does the perennial self-seed? As with self-seeding annuals, it depends on the location of the perennial as to whether self-seeding is a problem or not. Helleborus will self-seed quite readily in the proper conditions, but in one respect this is a help in filling in bare spots in the garden. If the self-seeding quality of a perennial does not suit your garden site, choose one that is self-contained, such as the primrose.

Minimizing care for perennials

Good soil preparation at planting time, essential for successful perennials, will reflect in lowering the maintenance demands of the plant. Deep, rich soil will allow adequate space for roots and will eliminate having to divide the perennial frequently. Try to prepare the soil to a depth of 10 to 12 inches. After adding soil conditioner, let the soil settle for two weeks or more. If it doesn't rain, water some so the plant will settle and eliminate any air pockets. Then you can do your planting.

After you have planted the perennials you are going to use, apply a mulch to keep weeds down, moisture in, and the soil conditioned. For example, if you have just planted a bed of primroses, scatter some shredded bark or other suitable mulching material around the primroses to keep them insulated.

Two undemanding chores need to be performed annually in a perennial garden. You'll need to spread around a complete fertilizer when growth starts in the spring, and you'll need to clip dead blossoms after the perennial has bloomed. If you have a row of agapanthus, merely go out with your clippers after the flowers have faded, leaving the barren seedheads, and clip them off. That is all there is to it until next year.

Depending on your climate, you may have to cover perennials slightly in the fall to protect them from freezing conditions. In very severe winters, cover perennials with straw, salt hay, or evergreen boughs in late fall. Often in the southern United States where winters are relatively mild, it helps to cover beds with a mulching material so that plants will remain dormant and not start to grow during warm spells, only to freeze during sudden cold snaps. When choosing perennials, use those that are very hardy in your area and do not need much protection.

NAME	HARDINESS ZONES	SUN OR SHADE	APPROX. HEIGHT	COMMENTS
ACANTHUS mollis BEAR'S BREECH	9-10	Shade	2-3 ft.	Spreading plant with long, glossy, deeply-lobed leaves. Lilac spikes bloom in early summer. Best in moist, shady spots.
ACHILLEA YARROW	4-10	Sun	3 ft.	Requires only routine care for generous summer, early fall bloom. Flower heads in flattish clusters of yellow or white.

LEFT: Contrasting with greenery is Centaurea cineraria *(Dusty miller).* **Center:** Campanula elatines garganica *(Bellflower) spills from crevice.* **Right:** Agapanthus *(Lily-of-the-Nile) in bloom.*

... Perennials (continued)

NAME	HARDINESS ZONES	SUN OR SHADE	APPROX. HEIGHT	COMMENTS
ANEMONE hupehensis japonica JAPANESE ANEMONE	6-10	Part shade	2-4 ft.	White pink, or rose flowers in fall. Slow to start; spreads when established.
AGAPANTHUS LILY-OF-THE-NILE	8-10	Sun-part shade	5 ft.	Blue, purple, or white flowers bloom in midsummer. Also dwarfs.
AQUILEGIA COLUMBINE	3-9	Sun	2-4 ft.	Spring, early summer bloom in pastels, deeper shades, or white. Tolerates filtered shade.
ARMERIA maritima COMMON THRIFT	6-10	Sun	6 in.	Tufted mounds of stiff, grasslike leaves. Profuse white to pink bloom.
ARTEMISIA	3-10	Sun	2-5 ft.	Silvery gray or white aromatic foliage good next to reds, oranges. Drought resistant.
ASPIDISTRA elatior CAST-IRON PLANT	8-10	Full-part shade	2 ft.	Glossy, veined leaves. Best in rich, porous soil.
ASTER frikartii	6-10	Sun	3-4 ft.	Abundant, lavender, fragrant flowers. Blooms almost all year in mild winter areas.
ASTILBE FALSE SPIRAEA, MEADOW SWEET	4-9	Sun-shade	6 in.-3 ft.	White, pink, or red plumelike flower clusters bloom May-July. Thrives in cool, moist soil.
BEGONIA semperflorens BEDDING BEGONIAS	9-10	Part shade	Varies by kind	Dwarf, intermediate, and tall types. Blooms all summer; grown as annuals in cold winter climates.
BELOPERONE guttata SHRIMP PLANT	8-10	Part shade	3-4 ft.	Flower resembles large shrimp. Pinch early growth for compact plant.
BERGENIA cordifolia HEARTLEAF BERGENIA	5-8	Part shade	20 in.	Spring-blooming rose or lilac flower clusters, roundish leaves. Takes neglect, poor soil, but responds to good soil, regular watering.

NAME	HARDINESS ZONES	SUN OR SHADE	APPROX. HEIGHT	COMMENTS
CAMPANULA BELLFLOWER	3-10	Sun-shade	4 in.-5 ft.	Nearly 300 species; flowers usually blue, bell-shaped.
CENTAUREA cineraria DUSTY MILLER	4-10	Sun	1 ft.	Purple or yellow flower heads on whitish foliage bloom in summer. Very hardy.
CHAMAEDOREA elegans	9-10	Shade	3-4 ft.	Slow-growing palm. Needs plenty of moisture, regular feeding.
CHRYSANTHEMUM frutescens MARGUERITE, PARIS DAISY	8-10	Sun	4 ft.	Abundant, daisylike flowers. Sensitive to cold. Replace every 2-3 years.
C. maximum SHASTA DAISY	6-10	Sun	2-4 ft.	Many varieties in white. Needs well-drained soil; accepts partial shade in hot climates.
C. parthenium FEVERFEW	6-10	Sun	1-3 ft.	Compact, aggressive, old-fashioned perennial.
COREOPSIS grandiflora	4-10	Sun	1-3 ft.	Large, bright yellow, orange flowers bloom all summer. Tends to self-sow.
DIANTHUS PINK, SWEET WILLIAM, CARNATION	4-10	Sun	4 in.-4 ft.	Over 300 species. Most form evergreen mats or tufts; fragrant bloom spring or summer.
DICENTRA BLEEDING HEART	4-8	Shade	8 in.-5 ft.	Short-lived in mild-winter areas, best in cold. Fernlike foliage dies down in winter. Dainty, spring-summer bloom.
DICTAMNUS albus GAS PLANT, FRAXINELLA	4-8	Sun-part shade	2½-4 ft.	Forms clump of olive green leaves; spikelike clusters of summer bloom. Long-lived in colder climates. Needs good soil.
DORONICUM LEOPARD'S BANE	4-8	Shade	2 ft.	Yellow, daisylike flowers rise from dark green leaf mounds in late spring. Needs good soil, dense shade.
EPIMEDIUM grandiflorum BISHOP'S HAT	4-8	Shade	12-15 in.	Leaflets bronzy pink in spring, green in summer, bronzy in fall. Tiny, pastel flowers in spring.
EUPHORBIA veneta SPURGE	6-10	Sun	4 in.-4 ft.	Shrubby perennials include poinsettias. Many succulent types, chartreuse blooms. Needs well-drained soil.
EURYOPS pectinatus	9-10	Sun	To 3 ft.	Daisylike flowers with long bloom season. Needs good drainage.
FELICIA amelloides BLUE MARGUERITE	8-10	Sun	1½ ft.	Produces almost continuous blue, yellow-centered daisies if dead flowers picked. Looks ragged if not severely pruned.
GAILLARDIA aristata COMMON BLANKET FLOWER	7-10	Sun	2-3 ft.	Long summer bloom season. Makes good cut flowers. Thrives in heat, takes some drought.
GYPSOPHILA paniculata BABY'S BREATH	3-9	Sun	3-4 ft.	Profuse tiny, white flowers. 'Bristol Fairy' is billowy.
HELICHRYSUM petiolatum	8-10	Sun	2 ft.	Mass of white, woolly leaves; good in sandy soils. Needs room.
HELIOPSIS scabra	4-8	Sun	3-4 ft.	Large, yellow flowers; several garden varieties. Blooms July to fall, dies back in winter.
HELLEBORUS niger CHRISTMAS ROSE	4-8	Shade	1½ ft.	Best in colder climates. Dark green leaves, white flowers.
H. orientalis LENTEN ROSE	6-9	Shade	1½ ft.	Greenish, purplish, or rose flowers often splashed with purple. Best in warm climates.
HEMEROCALLIS DAYLILY	3-10	Sun	1-6 ft.	Arching, sword-shaped leaves, lilylike flowers in tawny colors stand above foliage. Any soil; part shade in hot areas.

NAME	HARDINESS ZONES	SUN OR SHADE	APPROX. HEIGHT	COMMENTS
HEUCHERA sanguinea CORAL BELLS	5-10	Sun	14-24 in.	Compact leaf tufts, coral flower clusters bloom April-August. Tolerates most soil types.
HIBISCUS moscheutos PERENNIAL HIBISCUS, ROSE-MALLOW	5-10	Sun	6-8 ft.	Large red or white blooms from early June to frost. Plants die back in winter. Needs regular watering.
HOSTA PLANTAIN LILY	3-8	Sun-shade	3 ft.	Trumpet-shaped, lilac flowers rise from mounds of heart-shaped leaves. Dormant in winter. Clumps expand, shade out weeds.
HYSSOPUS officinalis HYSSOP	4-10	Sun	1½-2 ft.	Narrow, pungent leaves. Blue, pink, or white flower spikes late summer to fall.
IBERIS sempervirens EVERGREEN CANDYTUFT	5-10	Sun	3-18 in.	Clusters of white flowers in spring-early summer. Dark green leaves look good all year.
KNIPHOFIA uvaria RED-HOT POKER, TORCH-LILY, POKER PLANT	6-10	Sun	2-6 ft.	Dense clumps of grasslike leaves; pokerlike, orange-red or yellow flowers. Any soil; full sun.
LANTANA montevidensis	8-10	Sun	1 ft.	Clusters of lilac, pastel flowers bloom over long season. Thrives in heat; dies with frost but comes back. Any soil, needs spring pruning.
LAVANDULA spica ENGLISH LAVENDER	6-10	Sun	3-4 ft.	Lavender flowers, many dwarf varieties. Needs little water or fertilizer, good drainage.
LITHODORA diffusa	6-8	Sun	6-12 in.	Prostrate, mounded leaves sprinkled with tubular flowers of brilliant blue in early summer. Needs loose, well-drained soil.
LOTUS corniculatus BIRDSFOOT TREFOIL	6-9	Sun	2 ft.	Forms mat of dark, cloverlike leaves, clusters of small yellow flowers in summer and fall. Goes dormant in cold winters; needs plenty of water in hot, dry weather.
LUPINUS arboreus LUPINE	9-10	Sun	5-8 ft.	Yellow or lilac flower clusters in March-June. Any soil; requires good drainage.
LYTHRUM salicaria	3-10	Sun	2½-5 ft.	Showy, magenta-flowered plants in moist, sunny areas. Good cut flowers in late summer and fall.
MORAEA iridioides FORTNIGHT LILY, AFRICAN IRIS	8-10	Sun	4 ft.	Clumps of evergreen, irislike leaves. Grows from rhizomes, but stalks are perennial. 'Johnsonii' a robust variety.
PAEONIA HERBACEOUS PEONY	3-8	Sun	2-4 ft.	Spectacular spring bloom, needs a cold winter to perform well. Grows in almost any soil.
PAPAVER orientale ORIENTAL POPPY	3-8	Sun	4 ft.	Flowers in brilliant, pastel shades in spring. Short-lived in warm-winter climates. Requires ordinary soils, good drainage, no fertilizer.
PELARGONIUM hortorum COMMON GERANIUM	8-10	Sun	3 ft.	Summer blooms in pinks, reds, oranges. Tolerates most soils.
PHLOX	4-9	Sun	6 in.-4 ft.	Wide variety of growth forms, showy flower types. Takes light shade.
PHORMIUM tenax NEW ZEALAND FLAX	8-10	Sun	To 9 ft.	Bold plant with stiff, swordlike vertical leaves. Variants in leaf color available. Tolerates adverse conditions.
POLYSTICHUM setosum JAPANESE LACE FERN	7-10	Shade	2 ft.	Lacy, dense fern; fronds somewhat upright.
PULMONARIA saccharata BETHLEHEM SAGE	3-8	Shade	1½ ft.	White-spotted leaves; pink, violet, or white flowers.

NAME	HARDINESS ZONES	SUN OR SHADE	APPROX. HEIGHT	COMMENTS
RHOEO spathacea MOSES-IN-THE-CRADLE	9-10	Sun-Shade	1 ft.	Sword-shaped, dark green leaves with purple beneath.
STOKESIA laevis STOKES ASTER	6-10	Sun	1½-2 ft.	Blue or white flowers in summer, early autumn. Rugged and adaptable plant.
STRELITZIA reginae BIRD OF PARADISE	9-10	Sun	30 ft.	Tropical plant with huge, dramatic leaves.
THALICTRUM MEADOW RUE	3-10	Shade	3-6 ft.	Airy clusters of summer blooms in lavenders, white. Gives light shade, wind protection, ample moisture.

Bulbs...
the easiest of all

Few can deny the spiritual uplift that comes with the first splash of unexpected spring bulb colors. Crocus, daffodils, and tulips begin to appear during the first mild signs of spring. Often they pop up even under a thin layer of snow.

Bulbs have the delightful characteristic of being almost sure-fire performers. But since some need more care than others, it helps to know a few tricks in selecting the right bulbs for low maintenance.

Questions to ask about bulbs

A few questions have to be asked before you select bulbs for a low maintenance garden site. Carefully consider the following points:

Do the bulbs naturalize? Whether or not the bulbs will naturalize is probably the most important consideration in choosing bulbs for easy care. After you plant bulbs, you want to be able to leave them in the ground and not have to bother with them again. If you have to remove them from the ground, divide, and refrigerate them each year, then they are not worth the trouble and certainly should not be considered for a low maintenance garden. Generally, such bulbs as daffodils, crocus, iris, hyacinth, and muscari (grape hyacinth) can be left in the ground for a long period of time. If native bulb growth exists in your area, consider planting the natives; they will not have to be removed from the ground.

In some cases, bulbs will perform well for about five years and then will not produce as well as they did previously. In this case, you will have to lift and divide them if you want to continue to have good bloom. But five years of easy-care bulbs is not a bad average in a low maintenance garden.

What is the composition of the soil and the nature of the site you have chosen for bulbs? The ideal soil for most bulbs is one that is porous and drains well but holds water for the roots. Such a soil is generally rich in organic matter. If your soil is heavy clay and drains slowly or is very sandy and does not hold water, it can be improved by adding organic soil amendments—peat moss, ground bark, sawdust, or buckwheat hulls. Don't try planting bulbs in soil that always has poor drainage, for the bulbs will have a tendency to rot.

Does the bulb require staking? Tall-growing bulbs, such as gladiolus and lilies, often require staking or a fence to lean against, so consider this before you choose your bulbs. You probably won't want to be bothered by having to stake bulbs unless they are particular favorites of yours.

Is your climate compatible with bulb production? Generally, bulbs need a cold winter in order to produce the best flowers. In milder climates, bulbs are often refrigerated for a period of time before they are planted in order to artificially create the conditions that they need. Heat and high humidity decrease the life of the bulb, so you must consider your climatic conditions in relation to bulb culture. For example, tulips grow magnificently in the northern areas of the United States. But they have to be removed from the ground and refrigerated in order to do well in southern or mild areas.

Are rodents a problem in your area? Many bulbs are tasty morsels for burrowing gophers and other nuisance rodents. However, report has it that narcissus, because of their foul taste, tend to repel rodents. Some gardeners plant a ring of narcissus bulbs around garden areas to keep rodents out. If you have rodents, check with your county agricultural agent for the best methods to eradicate or discourage them.

Minimizing bulb care

Good soil and good drainage are prime requirements for healthy bulbs. If you provide the site you have chosen with proper drainage and soil rich in organic material, the bulbs should last a long period of time. Remember that most bulbs require sun at least half of the day. Dense shade is appropriate for only a few bulbs —among them crocus, scilla, and snowdrops.

Bulbs like to be fertilized just before they are ready to flower and again after they have bloomed so that energy and nutrients will go back into the bulb for proper flower production the following year. The easiest way to fertilize is to scatter a little fertilizer or bone meal around bulbs at appropriate times.

Don't cut bulb foliage away until it has turned yellow and dry. The nourishment of the leaves must be returned to the bulb for the development of next year's bloom. Again, this technique reemphasizes the importance of using informal areas for bulb culture so that fading foliage does not bother you. If you like annuals, you can always plant them in the bulb beds to cover up the fading foliage as the bulbs dwindle. Or you can place bulbs in beds of ground cover. A bed of bright yellow daffodils shooting up through a blue ajuga ground cover creates a sensational display of garden color.

Depending on the region where you live, you may need to mulch bulb beds. In cold, northern climates, you can mulch with straw, evergreen boughs or other appropriate material to prevent the ground from heaving during the winter months. Sometimes in the South, bulbs are covered to prevent premature growth during a warm winter spell.

You may have to do a little experimenting with bulbs in your garden. First, plant small clusters of various bulbs. When you find the ones that are at home, concentrate on planting them in mass.

NAME	HARDINESS ZONES	SUN OR SHADE	APPROX. HEIGHT	COMMENTS
AMARYLLIS belladonna BELLADONNA LILY, NAKED LADY	7-10	Sun	2-3 ft. by 2-3 ft.	Strap-shaped leaves in fall and winter die in summer, replaced by stalks topped with pink, trumpet-shaped flowers.
ANEMONE WINDFLOWER	4-10	Sun-Shade	6-14 in.	Choose the small, hardy woodland natives. Poppylike flowers in white, pink, blue variations.
BABIANA stricta BABOON FLOWER	7-10	Sun	6-12 in.	Blue, red, or cream flowers on spikes in May or June. Almost any soil, not much water.
CALADIUM bicolor FANCY-LEAFED CALADIUM	9-10	Sun	2-4 ft.	Large, arrow-shaped leaves in red, pink, white, silver, and green. Needs warmth.
CANNA	8-10	Shade	18 in. for dwarfs; others to 5 ft.	Tropical looking plants with lilylike flowers in an extensive color range. Best in rich, loose soil, heat.
CHIONODOXA luciliae GLORY-OF-THE-SNOW	4-9	Shade	6 in.	Blue and white starlike flowers among first to bloom in spring. Thrives in cold winters, half shade.
CLIVIA miniata KAFFIR LILY	9-10	Shade	1½-2 ft.	Brilliant orange blooms rise from clumps of dark green, strap-shaped leaves in spring. Needs warmth, moisture.
CONVALLARIA majalis LILY-OF-THE-VALLEY	3-8	Shade	6-8 in.	Small, drooping, white bell-shaped flowers. Ground cover in partial shade. Best in cold winter areas.
CRINUM VELD LILY	9-10	Part Shade	3 ft.	Mostly evergreen, thick, strap-shaped leaves; showy white or pink flowers in spring or summer.
CROCOSMIA crocosmaeflora MONTBRETIA	7-10	Sun	3-4 ft.	Sword-shaped leaves; orange, red, yellow flowers in summer. Spreads freely. Grows in part shade where hot.
CROCUS	3-9	Sun	3-6 in.	Wide variety of colors; showy in masses. Best adapted to colder climates.
CYCLAMEN	7-10	Shade	4-6 in.	Chose small-flowered hardy types for naturalizing. Long blooming season.
ERYTHRONIUM DOG-TOOTH VIOLET, FAWN LILY	3-8	Shade	8-15 in.	Dainty yellow, purple, or rose flowers bloom in spring. Likes cool, moist spots. Good for naturalizing in masses.
FREESIA	8-10	Sun	18 in.	Yellowish, fragrant flowers; hybrids in other colors.

LEFT: Evergreen clivia miniata *(Kaffir lily) blooms in shade.* **Center:** *Lavender* crocus tomasinianus *among juniper.*
Right: Narcissus 'Brunswick' (Daffodil) face sun, are cheery yellow touch.

NAME	HARDINESS ZONES	SUN OR SHADE	APPROX. HEIGHT	COMMENTS
GALANTHUS SNOW-DROP	5-9	Sun	12 in.	White, bell-shaped flowers best adapted to cold climates. One of the earliest spring bloomers. Easy to naturalize.
GLADIOLUS	8-10	Sun	6 ft.	Outstanding cut flowers in rich array of colors. Needs rich, sandy soil.
HEMEROCALLIS DAYLILY	3-10	Sun	1-6 ft.	Large clumps of arching, sword-shaped leaves, lily-like flowers in many colors. Adapts to almost any soil.
IRIS DUTCH IRIS	6-10	Sun	18-30 in.	Orchidlike flowers bloom March-April in mild winter areas, May-June in colder climates.
IXIA maculata AFRICAN CORN LILY	7-10	Sun	18-20 in.	Clusters of cup-shaped flowers in cream through yellow, orange, red and pink bloom May-June.
LYCORIS SPIDER LILY	4-10	Light shade	To 2 ft.	Clusters of red, pink, or yellow flowers in August-September. Should not be disturbed in ground.
MUSCARI GRAPE HYACINTH	3-9	Sun-shade	4-12 in.	Blue, spring flower clusters. Adapts to almost any soil. Light shade in warm climates, otherwise full sun.
NARCISSUS DAFFODIL	3-10	Sun	1 ft.	Adapts to many situations and soils; reliable, profuse spring bloom. 'King Alfred' a dependable variety.
NERINE	8-10	Sun	12-24 in.	Funnel-shaped, mostly pink or red blooms in fall. Blooms best when crowded.
SCILLA SQUILL, BLUEBELL	5-9	Shade	3-12 in.	Bell-shaped blooms in blue, purple, pink, white. *S. hispanica* is hardy, prolific, easy-to-grow.
TRILLIUM WAKE ROBIN	4-9	Shade	18 in.	Early spring maroon or white blooms. Good in woodsy, shady spot. Do not disturb rhizomes, will gradually increase.
TULIPA TULIP	3-8	Sun	40 in.	Wide variety of bright colors. Best in cold winters; sandy, well-drained soil.
ZANTEDESCHIA CALLA	8-10	Shade	4 ft.	Dark green leaf clumps, white flower bracts with yellow spike. Grows in shade, poor soil, boggy areas.
ZEPHYRANTHES ZEPHYR FLOWER, FAIRY LILY	7-10	Sun	8 in.	Graceful, funnel-shaped blossoms in late summer or fall. Easy to naturalize.

Index

Boldface numbers indicate chart entries.

Photographers

William Aplin: 13 top; 69 left, right; 74 middle; 82 right; 88 right. **Morley Baer:** 4-5. **Clyde Childress:** 12 bottom. **Glenn Christiansen:** 93 right. **Thomas P. Davidson:** 74 right. **Richard Dawson:** 5 top. **Chandler D. Fairbank:** 13. **Richard Fish:** 82 middle. **Jeanette Grossman:** 88 middle. **Hickey & Robertson:** 8 top. **George Hull:** 9 middle. **Elsa Knoll:** 85 right. **Sam Knoll:** 6 top right. **Ells Marugg:** 7 left, right; 10 bottom; 88 left; 93 left. **Rush J. McCoy:** 8 bottom. **Philip Molten:** 10 middle. **Don Normark:** 6 left; 9 bottom; 13 bottom; 82 left. **Photo Art Commercial Studio, Portland, Oregon:** 11 bottom. **Norman Plate:** 5 right. **John Robinson:** 85 middle. **Darrow M. Watt:** 6 bottom right; 9 top; 10 top; 11 top; 12 top; 69 middle; 74 left; 85 left. **Doug Wilson:** 93 top middle.